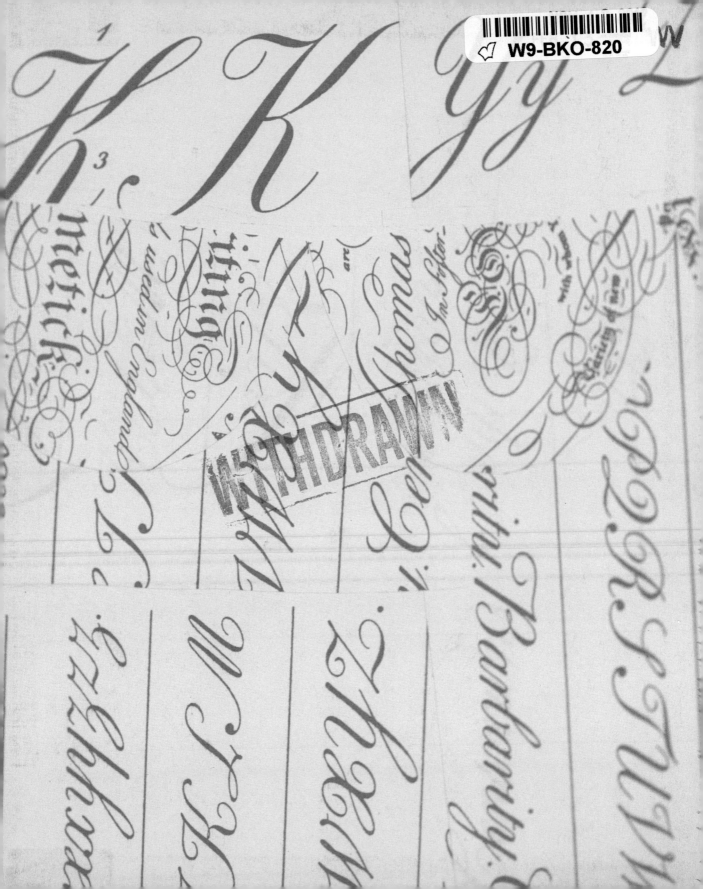

Book Art

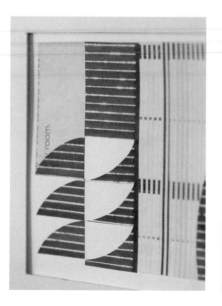

Book Art

Creative ideas to transform your books—
decorations, stationery, display scenes, and more

Clare Youngs

CICO BOOKS
LONDON NEW YORK

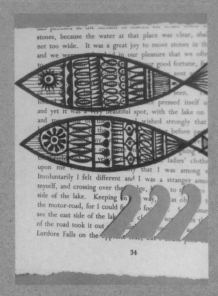

Published in 2012 by CICO Books
An imprint of Ryland Peters & Small Ltd
20–21 Jockey's Fields   519 Broadway, 5th Floor
London WC1R 4BW   New York, NY 10012

www.cicobooks.com

10 9 8 7 6 5 4 3 2 1

Text © Clare Youngs 2012
Design and photography © CICO Books 2012

A CIP catalog record for this book is available from the
Library of Congress and the British Library.

ISBN: 978 1 908170 92 7

Printed in China

Editor: Marilyn Inglis
Design: No Days Off
Photography: Caroline Arber
Illustration: Clare and Ian Youngs
Styling: Clare Youngs

Contents

Introduction

Looking through my own collection of books on the shelves in my studio, I realized that I love books for many different reasons. Besides the pleasure they give in the reading, and the information and facts I can glean from them, the graphic designer in me loves the layout, the different typefaces and ornate lettering, and the beautifully embossed covers (from the 19th century to the wonderful graphic covers of the 50s and 60s). I often buy old books purely for the cover and prop them up around the house to be admired as mini works of art. The artist and craftsman in me appreciates the feel of the book, the method of binding, and the textures and variety of paper from the translucent and thin to the luxuriously thick and creamy. I even like the smell of books, although I admit that it is a new book scent I like, rather than an old musty smell!

Books, without you even realizing, can make a huge and lasting impression. I know this because while researching this book in many wonderful old bookshops, I sometimes came across a book from my childhood. I may not have thought about that book for many, many years but, on opening the book, each illustration and the written text had been firmly planted in my mind. The happy childhood memories came flooding back.

So, if I love books so much, you may wonder how I am able to justify attacking them with a scalpel and a pair of scissors!

I have to admit that the first time I cut up a book it did not seem the right thing to do. However, that feeling of guilt dispersed as I began to create unique and beautiful objects from a simple page or group of pages.

Saying that, I do have my own book of rules that I have subconsciously set up. I do not cut up rare books. I seek out tatty and damaged books. I actually love finding an interesting book that has a few pages ruined by a child's scribbles, an ink stain, a missing cover, or torn pages. You don't even have to use old books; some of my favorite projects are made from the pages of old home wares catalogs. It is also a known fact that many thousands of books are pulped each year or end up in landfill. Being realistic, I know that some books do come to the end of their lives and lose relevance over the passage of time. But, by turning something into art that would otherwise be disregarded as rubbish, the forgotten pages are brought back to life, becoming part of the creations that add individuality and character to your home.

I respect books but, as a designer and craft-maker, I also believe that constructing something unique from the pages invites the same respect. It opens up the book to create new ideas, new fascination, and wonder. It invites new discussion, revives old memories, and creates new ones. So go and create!

A FU
watch the
nd our par
had no doubt
would have
r or no Tailbiter,
would have
mself,
upon its
What can I do
felt the answer
'Nothing,' it said.
You do not belong
As he climbed
does not

Cards & Stationery

Birdcage Cards

I rescued from the recycling bin a collection of old books that were falling apart and perfect for many of the projects in this book. One or two of the covers have lovely gold decoration or lettering that looks very pretty with the birdcage theme. Use a sharp blade in your craft knife since the front cover board in old books is very thick.

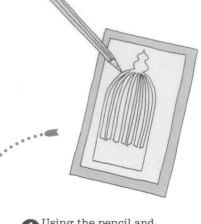

1 Using the pencil and tracing paper, trace around the birdcage template of your choice on page 118.

2 Position the trace on a page of text from the book so that the base of the birdcage is in the blank margin at the bottom of the page, and the rest of the birdcage is in the type. Use the craft knife to carefully cut out the birdcage.

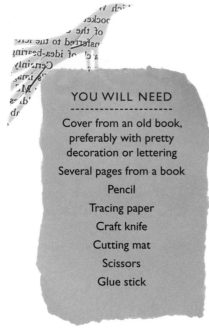

YOU WILL NEED

Cover from an old book, preferably with pretty decoration or lettering

Several pages from a book

Pencil

Tracing paper

Craft knife

Cutting mat

Scissors

Glue stick

3 To embellish the birdcage, choose one of the decorative templates from page 118. One design is a pattern to be cut out directly from the base of the birdcage, while the other two require a pattern to be cut from a section of text and stuck on. For the first alternative, trace the decorative pattern onto the base of the birdcage and, using the craft knife, cut out the pattern. For the second option, trace the decorative pattern from the template onto another page and, using the scissors and craft knife (see illustration right), cut out the pattern. Secure the pattern to the base of the birdcage with a dab of glue.

4 Place the cover on the cutting mat and, with a very sharp craft knife, cut out a decorative section from the front cover of the book (or use the whole thing).

5 Place the birdcage over the decorative lettering or motif, and secure with a few blobs of glue. Using the template from page 118, trace the bird with the pencil and tracing paper, transfer to a page of text, cut it out, and stick the bird into position with a bit of glue.

Cut-out Greetings Cards

Recently, I've been working on a series of artworks printed directly onto the pages of old books—I love the extra textural quality that comes from type on the page and the variations of cream-colored paper. In this project the page is the background and contrasts well with the strongly graphic element of the creatures.

YOU WILL NEED

Pages from an old book
Colored card stock
Pencil
Tracing paper
Black pen
Cutting mat
Craft knife
Ruler
Eraser
Kitchen knife
Glue stick

1 To make the rabbit card: using the pencil and tracing paper, trace the rabbit and wheat template (see page 118), and transfer these on to a page from the old book.

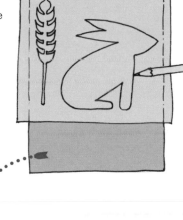

2 The templates for all three creatures are simply outlines, so that you can fill in each one with any pattern you like. Use the black pen to make patterns of circles, stripes, flowers, and swirls to fill the shape (use the photographs for inspiration if you like).

3 Place the page on the cutting mat and use the craft knife to cut out the wheat shape.

4 To make the roughly torn edge to the paper, first mark out in pencil a rectangle around the rabbit and wheat images. The rectangle should measure approx. 5 x 4in (12.5 x 10cm). Make sure that you center the image within the rectangle. Line up the ruler along one of the lines marking the side of the rectangle and tear away the paper up to the ruler. Do this to all four sides, then rub out any pencil marks that may be showing.

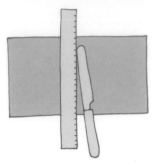

5 Take a piece of colored card stock measuring 12 x 6in (30 x 15cm). With the pencil, mark the middle point (at 6in/15cm) along the top and bottom edge of the card. Score a line down the middle of the card by lining the ruler up to the two pencil marks and running the back of a kitchen knife down the length of the ruler.

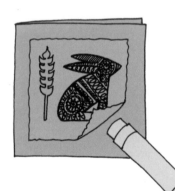

6 Fold the card stock in half along the scored line to make a 6 x 6in (15 x 15cm) card. Stick the page with the rabbit design onto the front of the folded card stock, centering the torn page on the square.

7 Repeat these steps for the snail and fish cards. The snail requires a slightly taller piece of paper, measuring approx. 5½ x 4in (14 x 10cm). The width is the same as the rabbit so you will need a piece of colored card stock measuring 12 x 7in (30 x 18cm) to fold in half.

THE SILENT TRAVELLER

Little Bird Prints

I came across a book of Japanese prose with beautiful lettering on old cream-colored paper. The pages of text make great backgrounds for stamped images and inspired me to create these little packets with a Japanese feel. Once you have cut out the rubber stamps from erasers, these are quick to create and make wonderfully special envelopes or packets for small gifts. Or why not make beautiful greetings cards by sticking the printed and torn-out rectangles onto some folded card?

1 To make the rubber stamps: using the soft pencil and tracing paper, trace the bird and the nest from the templates on page 118. Press both the erasers down in turn onto the traces so that the designs are transferred onto the surface of the erasers. Go over the lines with a sharp pencil to make the lines clearer.

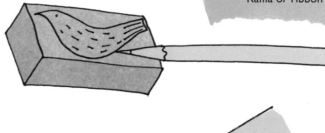

2 Cut around the shape of the bird using the craft knife.

3 Cut the design into the surface of the bird using the lino-cutting tool; go very gently and try not to dig too deeply. Cut out the nest in the same way.

4 Using pages of text from the book, tear out some paper measuring approx. 7 x 4in (18 x 10cm), following the instructions for making ragged-edged tears given in the Cutout Greetings Cards project on page 13.

5 Cut another stamp from a thin sliver of eraser in order to print the branches. On the torn piece of paper, print a series of branched twigs to form the larger branches (see illustration 6 for guidance). Use tiny pieces of eraser and a contrasting color of stamp pad to print some flowers on the branches.

6 Print two branches, one above the other. Print the nest and bird, positioning the nest on one of the branches.

7 To make a simple packet: take a letter-sized piece of colored paper (roughly 8¼ x 11¾in/21 x 30cm). Fold in 1in (2.5cm) on both long sides of the sheet of paper.

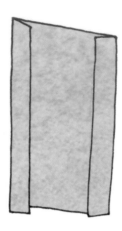

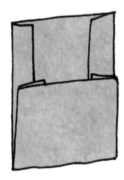

8 Fold over a flap approx. 4¾in (12cm) from the end of the rectangle, keeping the side folds inside the packet.

9 Fold over the top section to create the overlapping flap to the packet. Wrap the printed page around the packet (see photograph for guidance) and secure with some brightly colored raffia or ribbon. You can add other layers of textured paper before tying the bundle together, if you like.

は學の價值のものに依存す

これは正しい考へである思ふ。

正な

決してやむ決して止まぬ衷心から要求に

手段のみが如き場合は利用をを目的として學其のものを掴まんとする自發的精神に進んで自發的研

まれても其の通りであって本當の本當の心から何等か他の目的のため目的のための物理學を學し學居

るこれは正して其のあるもあるものはを決しな何等の要求の

り自己の趣向すべきところを知るために必要

である両者は其の態度に於て異なって居事は先

読書其のものは學ではない固より者は先

るものであるけれども其のため読書を以て

一視する事は出來ないましてや然として多

は精神のを妨げ思索を慢せしめる恐

來屢々多読がめられた所以であり併しながら

きを得て讀の沈溺する事は學のものの性

い事であるこれ昔ら読書を貴

い事であるこれ昔ら読書を貴

Japanese Notebook

All the designs in this book started life as a series of notes and drawings in small sketch books. I like to use small books I can pop into my bag so that they are handy when creative inspiration strikes! Home-made books make lovely presents and you can personalize the cover with anything. I found an old street map of London and, although a few pages were spoiled by a large ink stain, the rest of the book was a gem that went perfectly with my collection of old maps.

1 Decide on the dimensions of your notebook. You can make different sizes but if you keep the width to 4⅜in (11cm), the holes can be evenly spaced. Cut out some pages of blank paper and two pieces of thin card stock to the size you have chosen.

2 Stack the paper and the thin card stock together to form your notebook. Mark in pencil the position of the holes. Place the row of holes ⅝in (1.5cm) from the spine edge. Using the ruler, mark the first hole ⅝in (1.5cm) from the side edge of the cover. Space the next four holes ¾in (2cm) apart, which will leave you a ⅝in (1.5cm) space at the other end.

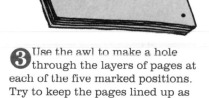

3 Use the awl to make a hole through the layers of pages at each of the five marked positions. Try to keep the pages lined up as you work.

4 Thread the needle with approx. 32in (80cm) of waxed thread or twine. Start at the third hole, lift up a few pages, and thread the needle through the hole to come out at the front of the cover. Pull the thread through and leave 1in (2.5cm) of thread lying along the spine in between the pages.

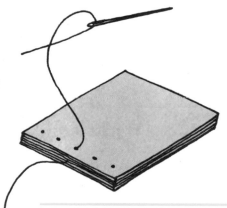

5 Take the needle down through the fourth hole, around the spine and back through the hole again. You may have to push the awl through the hole again to make it big enough.

6 Bring the needle up though the fifth hole, take it around the spine and up through the fifth hole again.

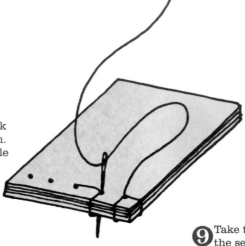

7 Take the needle around the edge of the book and bring it up through the fifth hole again. Move back to the fourth hole and take the needle back through it.

8 Bring the needle up through the third hole, around the spine and back through the third hole again.

9 Take the needle through the second hole, around the spine, and back up though the second hole again.

10 Take the needle up through the first hole around the edge of the spine and up through the first hole again. Take the needle around the edge of the book and bring it up through the first hole again.

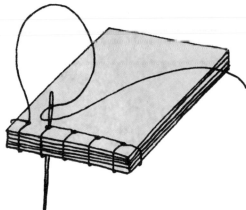

⑫ Take the needle along to the center hole. Place the needle under the threads going into the third hole. Pull it through to make a loop. Take the needle back through the loop to form a knot. Take the needle back through the third hole and cut off any left-over cotton flush with the cover (note that the illustration now shows the back view of the book).

⑪ Take the needle down through the second hole.

⑬ Decorate the front of the book by using the craft knife to cut an image the same size as the cover minus ¾in (2cm) for the spine. Stick down in position with the glue.

Pigeon Message Card

The greeting card industry is huge and the variety overwhelming, but everyone loves to receive a home-made card. It shows how much you really care and when they are simple to make like this little bird, there is no excuse! A rolled-up piece of paper around the leg of this pigeon holds a secret message to someone special.

YOU WILL NEED

Thin card stock

Pages from an illustrated book
(I found some old pictures
of London, perfect for pigeons)

Glue and a glue stick

Pencil

Tracing paper

Craft knife

Cutting mat

Quilling tool

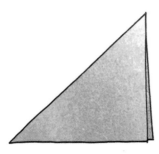

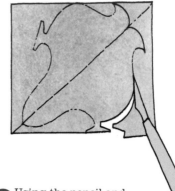

1 Cut out a square of thin card stock measuring 7⅓ x 7⅓ in (19 x 19cm). Score a line from one corner to the opposite corner and fold the card in half (see page 117 for instruction on scoring).

2 Using the glue stick, glue a picture from your illustrated book over one side of the triangle.

3 Using the pencil and tracing paper, trace the pigeon shape from the template on page 118 and transfer the pigeon shape onto the plain inside of the folded card. Cut out the pigeon shape using the craft knife and cutting mat.

4 Cut out a small circle of darker paper for an eye and stick it down with the glue.

5 To make the secret message scroll: cut a strip of paper measuring ¼in x 5in (5mm x 12cm). Use the quilling tool to roll it up into a tight coil (see the Whirlygig Brooch project on page 84 for how to use a quilling tool). Stick the end to the leg of the pigeon.

The Tower Bridge

Anna X

Pineapple

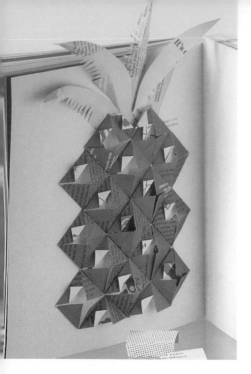

I made this pineapple to be displayed in an open book, but it would also make a wonderful greeting card. Make the squares for the body of the pineapple and the leaves slightly smaller and stick to folded thin card stock.

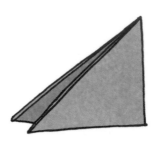

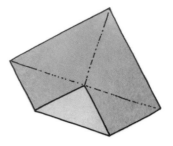

YOU WILL NEED

Pages from a book

Pencil

Tracing paper

Scissors

Craft knife

Cutting mat

Glue

Yellow paper (optional)

1 Using pages of one color from the book, cut 17 squares of paper measuring 1⅛ x 1⅛in (4 x 4cm). Fold each one in half to make a triangle and then in half again. This marks the center of the squares. Open up the squares of paper again.

2 Place one square in front of you, flat on the table, with a corner point facing toward you. Fold up one corner point to the center point and press the crease down flat with your fingers.

3 Repeat with the other three corners. Take one of the corners and fold back the tip of paper so that it lines up with the edge of the square. Repeat these steps on all 17 squares.

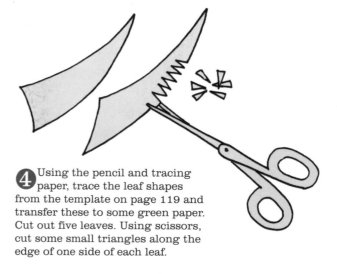

4 Using the pencil and tracing paper, trace the leaf shapes from the template on page 119 and transfer these to some green paper. Cut out five leaves. Using scissors, cut some small triangles along the edge of one side of each leaf.

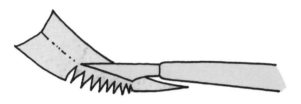

5 Score each leaf with the craft knife (see page 117 for detailed instructions on scoring). Take the blade very gently from the wide end of the leaf, curving the blade around to finish at the tip of the leaf. Don't press too hard; you need to just break the surface of the paper. Crease the leaves into a 3-D shape.

6 Place all the squares roughly on the page in position before you start gluing them down. Start with two squares next to each other, corner to corner, with the folded triangles facing left.

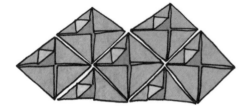

7 Place the next row, made up of three squares, in position below the first row, lining up to the sides of the two above. Carry on alternating rows of two squares, then three squares, ending with a row of three.

8 Cut the remaining two squares in half to make triangles to fill the gaps at the top and bottom of the pineapple (you will have one triangle left over). When you are happy with the arrangement you can glue all the squares down to the page or to some card stock if you are making a greeting card.

9 Arrange the leaves at the top of the pineapple and stick these down.

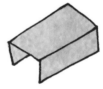

10 To make some pineapple chunks, cut a rectangle of yellow paper measuring 1½ x 1in (4 x 2.5cm). Crease and fold back ½in (1cm) on each side of the rectangle.

Covered Buttons

These pretty buttons are not really suitable to sew onto clothes but they do make lovely and unusual cards. Look out for larger buttons in thrift stores—these need to have a central button shank and measure about 1in (2.5cm) in diameter.

1 Using pages from old books, draw the same number of circles as you have buttons. When drawing the circles, make sure that you position the image in the center. You can either use a compass and pencil to make your circles, or draw around an object that is slightly larger than your button, but keep in mind that it must be larger than your button. For a 1in (2.5cm) button, the circle should measure 1½in (4cm) across. Cut out each circle of paper.

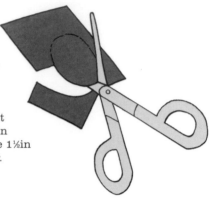

2 Spread some glue on the wrong side of the paper circle and place the button face-down in the center of the circle.

3 Start smoothing down the glued circle over the curve of the button. Make small snips around the edge of the circle to help you smooth out any creases. Tuck the overlapping bits to stick to the underside of the button.

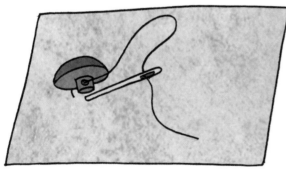

4 To make a card: cut two pieces of thin card stock measuring 5 x 3in (12.5 x 8cm). Position the buttons on one piece of card, then sew these in place using the needle and thread. Spread glue over the second piece of card and stick to the back of the first card to cover your stitching.

2

Decorating
The Home

Apples and Pears

These fruity shapes are easy to make and look beautiful arranged along a child's shelf or table. As children grow out of their first books, there are some favorites you will always want to keep, but others may be a little too well loved with pages torn or a cover missing. Transform these much-loved friends into apples and pears—and continue to enjoy them for years to come.

YOU WILL NEED

Old book without its cover

Pencil

Tracing paper

Cutting mat

Craft knife

Glue and a glue stick

1 To make the pear, take a section of the old book measuring approx. ½in (1cm) across the spine.

2 Using the template on page 119, trace the shape of the half pear onto tracing paper using the pencil. Transfer the shape onto the book section, making sure that the straight part of the trace is on the folded spine section of the book. Using the templates, trace two leaves and a stalk, and then set these aside.

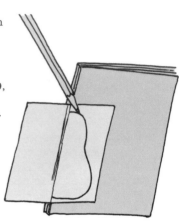

3 Put the book section on the cutting mat and, with the craft knife, cut out the half-pear shape, making sure that you cut through all the pages of the book.

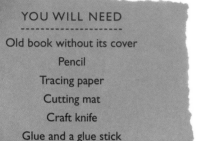

4 Fan out the half-pear shape to make a complete pear form. Put some dabs of glue along the edges of the first page and stick it to the last page to secure the shape in place.

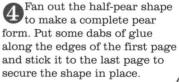
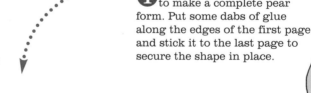

5 Using the traced templates, cut out two leaves and a stalk from another page of the book. Position the stalk between a couple of the pages at the top center of the pear and secure with a blob of glue. Do the same with the two leaves, one on either side of the stalk. To make the apple, follow exactly the same method as the pear.

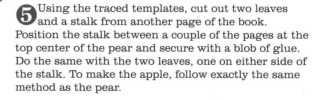

Paper Artichokes

I am constantly amazed by the versatility of a simple piece of paper—you can make it into practically anything. Admiring some artichokes in a bowl, I thought how beautiful they looked and wondered if I could capture them in paper. They turned out to be quite easy to make and quite beautiful too.

1 Using the pencil, tracing paper, and the template on page 119, trace and then transfer, and cut out leaves in different sizes from the pages of the old books. You will need some large leaves, approx. 2¾in (7cm) long; some medium ones, 2in (5cm) long; and some measuring 1¼in (3cm) long. You should be able to cut four or five leaves at the same time. When you get used to the shape you may be able to cut out the leaves without the template—it is nice to have some variation.

2 Starting with the smallest leaves, fold each leaf in half lengthwise, then open it out again, leaving a sharp crease down the middle.

3 Place a blob of glue at the base of the leaf and stick it in position at the top of the ball. Continue to stick small leaves all around the top of the ball, overlapping them as you go. Carry on around and down the ball for several rows, then move on to the medium-sized leaves, folding first, then gluing in place for several rows.

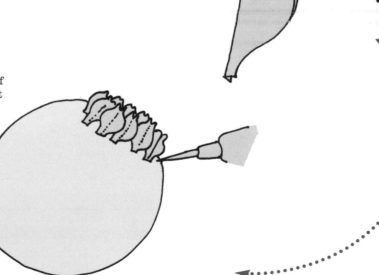

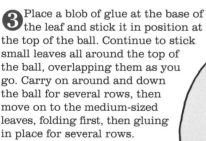

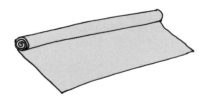

4 When you are about half-way down the ball, switch to the larger (already folded) leaves. Before gluing the larger leaves to the ball, however, make a small pleat at the stem of the leaf so that it becomes more three-dimensional and will stick out from the ball. Carry on down the ball, ending with a row of medium and then a row of small leaves at the bottom. Leave free of leaves a small area approx. ½in (1cm) wide at the base for the stem.

5 To make the artichoke stem, cut a strip 3in (8cm) wide from a page of the book. Start rolling it up tightly, adding a few blobs of glue as you go. The stem should be approx. ½in (1cm) thick, so add more strips of paper until you have the required thickness.

6 With the points of your scissors, dig out a bit of polystyrene from the clear area at the base of the artichoke. Put a blob of glue on one end of the stalk and push it into the hollowed-out area, placing it at an angle. Trim the end of the stalk at an angle to finish.

Paper Houses

The houses in this little scene are made from a simple box shape with an added roof. The design is easy to adapt so that you can make houses of any shape or size.

YOU WILL NEED

Pages from books

Pencil

Craft knife

Cutting mat

Blunt knife

Ruler

Glue

Tracing paper

Black pen

Eraser

Green ink pad
or green paint

1 To make the house: take a piece of paper measuring 7 x 8¼in (18 x 21cm) and with the pencil mark out a 1½in (4cm) border around all four sides. Using the craft knife, make a small slit at each of the four corners from the drawn rectangle out to the edge of the paper.

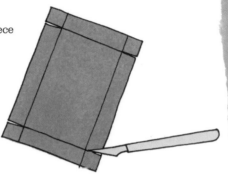

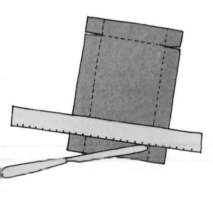

2 Using the back of the blunt knife and the ruler, score all the lines of the drawn rectangle, continuing the longer side lines up to the top of the page and down to the bottom (see page 117 for more details on scoring).

3 Using the ruler and pencil, draw rectangles for windows, measuring ¾ x 1½in (2 x 4cm). Position the top two windows ½in (1cm) in from the sides of the drawn rectangle and ¾in (2cm) from the top edge. Position the lower two windows underneath these, leaving a ⅝in (1.5cm) gap. Mark a rectangle for the door, measuring ¾ x 1in (2 x 2.5cm), centered along the bottom drawn edge of the rectangle. If you have made taller or wider houses you can add more windows.

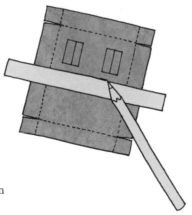

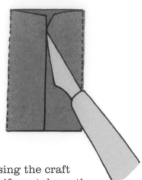

4 Using the craft knife, cut down the middle and across the top and bottom of each window rectangle. Score down the sides of each window rectangle using the blunt side of the kitchen knife. For the door, score down one long side and cut the other three sides of the rectangle.

5 Crease the score lines at the corners of the paper to raise up the sides of the box shape. Fold in each scored corner piece. These are the glue flaps. Glue the flaps to the inner side edges.

6 Cut out a roof shape using a contrasting color. This can be any size, but make sure that the base of the roof is ¾in (2cm) wider than the width of the house. You can add some decoration with scalloped rows of paper if you like. Stick the roof to the front of the house.

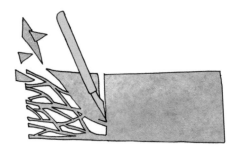

7 To make the trees: using the pencil and tracing paper, trace the trees from the templates on page 119 and transfer onto two pieces of paper from a book. Try to find thick paper so that they stand up well. For the drawn tree, position the image to the left edge of a piece of paper measuring 4 x 6¼in (10 x 16cm). Draw in over the pencil with black ink. Cut out a few leaf shapes using the craft knife. Score a line 1in (2.5cm) in from the left edge and crease back to make a stand.

8 For the cut-out tree: transfer the trace onto the left edge of a piece of paper measuring 2½ x 8¼in (6 x 21cm). Trace down to 2¾in (7cm). Cut out in between the branches and across the width of the oblong at the bottom of the drawn-in branches.

9 Score a line down the tree side of the paper ¾in (2cm) away from the edge. Bend back to make a stand.

10 To make the leaf shape for the bush, follow the directions on cutting a stamp from an eraser in the Little Bird Prints project on page 15. Using a pencil and tracing paper, trace the leaf shapes from the template on page 119 and transfer these to the eraser. Print three leaf shapes together, cut out the shape, and stick it to the edge of the house.

39

Rose Decoration

The book I used to make this paper rose is missing its cover and the pages are battered, but it holds special memories from my childhood and I have since shared it with my own children. Recently, I found a copy in good condition in a thrift shop so I knew I could use some of the pages from my damaged edition for a few of the projects. The soft, subtle colors make it ideal for this pretty paper flower.

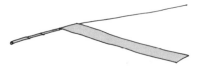

1 To make the stem: cut some wire approx. 9in (23cm) long. Cut narrow strips of paper approx. ½in (1cm) wide from the pages of the book and run a glue stick along the length of paper. Wind the strips around and along the length of the wire to cover it.

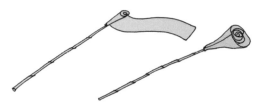

2 To make the center of the rose: cut a strip of paper approx. 1⅜in (3.5cm) wide. Place some glue along the lower edge of the strip and wind it around the top of the wire stalk. Try to keep the center tight for a few turns, then loosen the strip slightly as you wind, sticking the lower edge a tiny bit farther down the stalk as you wind.

3 To make the petals: use the pencil, tracing paper, and the template on page 119 to trace the shapes, then transfer these onto the pages from the book. Vary the sizes of the petals, making some wider and some smaller. Cut out the petals using the scissors.

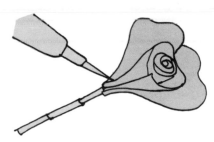

4 Starting with the smaller petals, place a dab of glue at the base of the petal and stick it in position, lining up the base of the petals with the bottom edge of the rose center. Continue adding petals, increasing in size toward the outer edge. Use your fingers to curl the tips and sides of the petals slightly.

5 Using the pencil, tracing paper, and the template on page 119, trace a few leaf shapes, then transfer and cut these from pages of the book. Place a blob of glue at the base of the leaves and stick these to the stalk.

Sculptural Shapes

Transform some pages from an old book into these wonderfully curvy, sculptural forms. Surprisingly easy to make, you can cut these shapes to different heights and group them together for an unusual and striking display.

YOU WILL NEED

Some old books
Pencil
Tracing paper
Cutting mat
Craft knife
Glue stick

1 Remove the cover from an old book and divide the book into sections (the spine width of each section should be ½–¾in (1–2cm). Using the pencil and tracing paper, trace one of the templates from page 120, then transfer the shape onto the first page of a section.

2 Put the book section on your cutting mat and, using the craft knife, cut through all the pages following your traced outline.

3 Fan out the pages to make the three-dimensional shape. Glue the first and last pages together to secure the shape in place.

4 For an alternative shape, use template 3 on page 120 and follow steps 1 and 2 to cut out this shape. Once you have completely cut out the new shape, fold in the protruding curved portion of the shape so that the tip of the curve touches the spine. Repeat this folding process on each page.

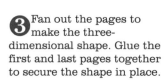

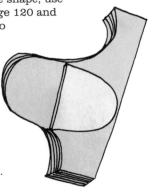

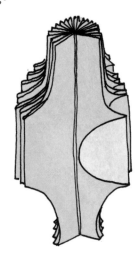

5 Fan the pages around and glue the first and last pages together to secure the shape in place.

Winter Village Scene

I spotted this cheery, bright red, covered book in a flea market while rummaging in boxes of rather worn-out and tired books. The subject of the little red book was Christmas, so I knew it was perfect for this winter scene. I've made one for my mantelpiece and, when surrounded by pine cones and candlelight, it takes on a magical, fairytale appearance.

1 Using the pencil and tracing paper, trace the row of houses from the template on page 120 and transfer these to one of the pages in your book. Position the base of the houses along the edge of the type.

2 Place the cutting mat under the page and, using a craft knife, carefully cut out the houses, windows, and doors. Note the difference between cutting lines and dotted lines that indicate a fold.

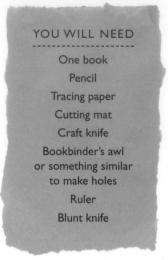

3 For the row of trees: repeat steps 1 and 2 on the other side of the book. Trace the trees from the template on page 120 and transfer to the opposite page behind the houses. Position the base of the trees along the edge of the type closest to the spine of the book. Once you have cut out the trees, make holes with the awl at the end of each large branch as decoration.

4 Position the ruler along the base of your cut-out scenes and gently score the paper with the back of a blunt knife. Fold up the rows of houses and trees along the scored line so they are standing out from the page. Finally, fold open the doors and windows to finish.

DECORATING THE HOME ✱

Pop-up Flowers Book

The great thing about creating projects for this book is that they don't have to be useful; they can be purely beautiful, and made just to be looked at and admired. This is just such a project and, although it looks very complicated and clever, it is, in fact, easy to make.

YOU WILL NEED

Suitable book
(I have used a paperback
brochure-type book)

Pages from books, both text
and colorfully illustrated

Thin card stock from the
cover of a paperback book

Pencil

Tracing paper

Craft knife

Cutting mat

Quick-drying strong glue

1 Using the pencil, tracing paper, and the template on page 120, trace the flower shape. Transfer the flower onto a thin piece of card stock and cut it out to create your master flower template. You can then draw around this master template to make a pile of flowers. Cut some from text pages only, some in muted colors, and others in bright colors. The idea is that the flowers emerge from the book page and gradually change to bright colors.

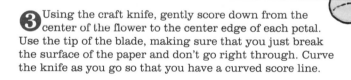

2 For each flower piece, cut out the two slots that will become the stamens of the flower, leaving the bottom of the slot intact.

3 Using the craft knife, gently score down from the center of the flower to the center edge of each petal. Use the tip of the blade, making sure that you just break the surface of the paper and don't go right through. Curve the knife as you go so that you have a curved score line.

4 To finish the flower, raise up the two center slots (for stamens) and then gently pinch each petal along the score lines to give the flowers a three-dimensional look.

5 Slide your cutting mat under one of the pages of your book. Using the master flower template and starting in the left-hand corner of the open book, trace the parts of the flowers to be cut from the page.

6 Using your craft knife, cut out just three petals of the first flower you've traced in the book. Score the three petals and pinch along the score lines to lift these from the surface. Position the second flower a little farther back and toward the right. On this flower, cut out three and a half petals and one of the center slots. Score and fold as before. Position the third flower farther back on the page, cut out four petals, and both of the slots. Score and fold as before.

7 Behind and next to this last cut flower, stick a few of your already-made text-only flowers. Paste the first one lying flat, and the others held by a blob of glue on just one of the petals (so that you can lift them up from the surface of the page), score, and fold.

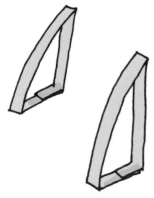

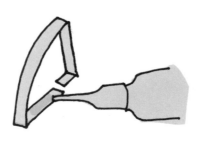

8 Continue the progression of flowers onto the rest of the open book, progressing from pale to bright colors. You need to lift them from the page and gradually increase the height as you go back across the page. To make the supports, take some strips of thin card stock and fold into triangles with the base of the triangle as the smallest side, and the front-facing side longer than the third side so that it curves. Make sure you leave an extra tab at the end to glue the triangle together. Make a few triangles in different heights.

9 Stick a prepared flower to the top of the curved side of the triangle support and glue the base in position behind the first few flowers.

10 Carry on adding flowers and supports, moving back toward the spine. When you attach flowers to the opposite page, the supports will need to be shorter, since you already have some height from the raised half of the book. This project requires you to use your judgment for the height of the supports. Try to position the flowers so that their supports are concealed by the flowers in front of them.

Abstract Cut-outs

I made these contemporary abstract artworks from the pages of an interior design catalog. From a distance they could be screen prints but, on close inspection, you can see the lettering and page numbers and the cut paper. There are three different templates but I have used a similar color palette so that they become a set when framed and hung together. Experiment with shapes and color combinations for different looks.

YOU WILL NEED

Pages from a catalog

White cartridge paper

Pencil

Tracing paper

Cutting mat

Craft knife

Ruler

Glue stick

1 Using the pencil and tracing paper, trace the abstract shapes from the templates on page 120. Use the traced shapes to cut out different sections from the pages of the catalog. Look out for catalogs printed on matt paper since the colors of these are usually good. Carefully cut out the sections on the cutting mat using the craft knife. On all three templates, part of the pattern cut away is also used to make a reverse image.

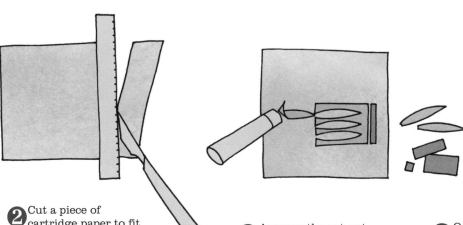

2 Cut a piece of cartridge paper to fit the frame you are using. I have used a 9in (23cm) square frame so my cartridge paper is that size but you can use different-sized frames with a smaller or larger border.

3 Arrange the cut-out sections on the cartridge paper, making sure that it is approximately in the middle of the paper and there is a white border all around the arrangement.

4 Once you are happy with the arrangement, you can stick the shapes down. Your artwork is ready to frame now. Repeat steps 2, 3, and 4 to make the other two artworks.

Paper-covered Wardrobe

Having recently moved and renovated an old house, we bought this old wardrobe for one of the bedrooms. Since it was a bit battered and not really a very nice color, I gave it a fresh coat of paint and came up with a dress and coathanger design to go on the door. The dress is made out of paper with wonderfully elegant script lettering that fits perfectly with the vintage style of the room but, if you can't find any script lettering, music score sheets would work as well.

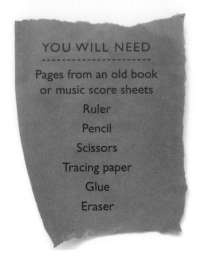

YOU WILL NEED

Pages from an old book
or music score sheets

Ruler

Pencil

Scissors

Tracing paper

Glue

Eraser

1 Because this project is so big, I have used the grid method for enlarging the image. This involves drawing a grid onto the wardrobe and drawing in the design, using the template on page 120. Each ½in (1cm) square on the template is equal to a 2¾in (7cm) square on the wardrobe. Start by drawing a rectangle in pencil on the wardrobe measuring 16½in (42cm) wide and 36in (92cm) long, divided into 6 squares across and 13 squares down. My wardrobe has a curve at the top so I started the measurement from the top center of the curve. Only part of the squares along the top row will be showing, but that's okay since the only drawing required there is the end of the pretend coathanger.

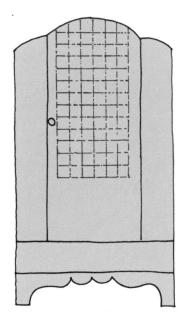

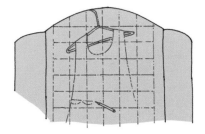

2 Following the template on page 120, and starting at the top of the grid, draw in the part of the design you see in each square of the template onto the corresponding square on the wardrobe. Don't worry about getting it exactly the same. The coathanger and top of the dress are the most difficult parts to draw. For the main part of the dress you don't have to follow the grid so carefully.

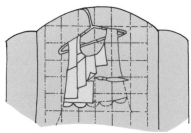

3 Start cutting out pieces of pages to glue in the dress area. You can overlap areas of type; just make sure that the cut-out bits of paper don't go over the pencil line of the dress.

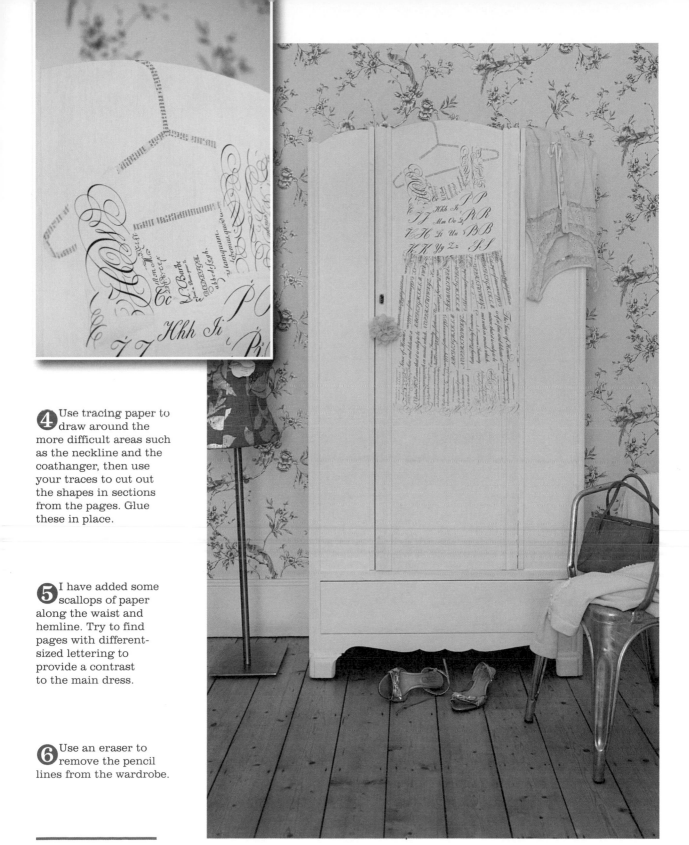

4 Use tracing paper to draw around the more difficult areas such as the neckline and the coathanger, then use your traces to cut out the shapes in sections from the pages. Glue these in place.

5 I have added some scallops of paper along the waist and hemline. Try to find pages with different-sized lettering to provide a contrast to the main dress.

6 Use an eraser to remove the pencil lines from the wardrobe.

Paper Bowls

These little bowls take some time to make but are well worth the effort. They are quite beautiful to look at, like mini sculptures—you want to pick them up as you would found objects such as pretty pebbles or shells. I have used matt pages from an interiors magazine in subtle grays, browns, and blues for the main body of the bowls, while the last strip around the rim is paper in blocks of color from the same brochure to add a splash of vibrancy.

YOU WILL NEED
- - - - - - - - - - - - - - - - - - - -
Pages from a brochure
or magazine

Ruler

Pencil

Cutting mat

Craft knife

Glue stick

❶ Start by cutting lots of strips of paper from the pages, making the strips all the same length and ⅝in (1.5cm) wide. Fold each strip in half lengthwise.

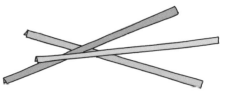

❷ To make the base, take the first strip of paper, run a glue stick along its length, and start winding it up tightly to make a flat coil. When you have finished one strip, repeat the process, adding more strips of paper and keeping the fold at the top edge of the coil.

❸ When the base reaches the width required, you can start building up the sides. The taller bowl I made has a 1½in- (4cm-) wide base and the other two bowls have 2in (5cm) and 2¾in (7cm) bases. When you start building up the sides, turn the strips up so that the fold is facing downward. As you wind a new strip around, place each new strip only a tiny fraction up from the base of the previous strip (about ⅛in/2mm). You can place the strips farther up, but if you are patient and build the sides up slowly, you will achieve a beautiful finish.

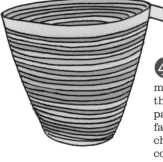

❹ Carry on until you reach the desired height. The last strip makes the rim of the bowl; therefore, reverse the strip of paper again so that the fold is facing upward. You might like to choose paper with a good strong color to finish off your bowl.

Hanging Tassels Decorations

These delicate baubles would be lovely to make at Christmas. Hang them on painted silver and white twigs for a pretty and unusual festive display.

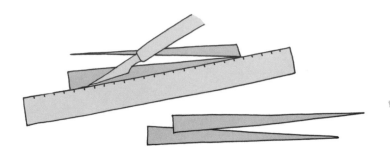

YOU WILL NEED

Pages from an old book (try to find thick paper for this project)

Cutting mat

Craft knife

Pencil

Ruler

Wire cutters

Glue stick and glue

Bookbinder's awl or something with a sharp point such as a compass or metal skewer

Thin wire (florists' or craft wire)

Scissors

Pair of pliers

1 First make some paper beads. For one of the larger beads, cut a strip of paper the length of the page and ¾in (2cm) wide. At one end of the strip make a pencil mark ½in (1cm) in from the edge to mark the middle. With a ruler, join the top corner at the end of the strip to the pencil mark. Cut this section away and repeat on the other side to make a triangle.

2 Run the glue stick along the length of the triangle. Roll up the triangle starting at the wide end and keeping the roll tight. You can vary the width of the triangles in order to get different-shaped beads.

3 Cut a strip of paper 1½in (4cm) wide. Glue and roll it tightly in the same way as step 2. Using the craft knife, slice it into small sections measuring ¼in (5mm) wide. These small beads are used to hold the strips of paper on the decoration in place.

4 To make the bauble shape: cut out 15 strips of paper ⅝ x 6in (1.5 x 15cm). Using the awl or other sharp point, make a small hole in the top of the strips, centered and approx. ⅜in (8mm) from the edge. Place the strips together when making the holes so that the holes are in the same position on each strip. Repeat this at the other end of the strips.

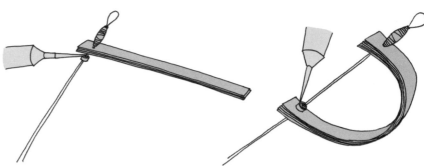

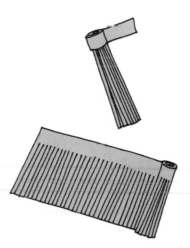

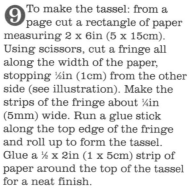

5 Take a thin piece of wire, approx. 12in (30cm) long, and fold it in half. Thread a larger bead onto the folded wire. You can push your sharp point through the bead first to make it easier. Position the bead about ⅝in (1.5 cm) from the end of the folded wire. Open out the loop of wire into a circular shape to stop the bead moving up any farther.

6 Thread all 15 strips of paper onto the folded wire. Take one of the small beads cut from the roll, thread it onto the wire, and push it up close to the strip of paper. Place a blob of glue on the end of the bead to secure it to the bottom strip of paper.

7 Thread another small bead onto the folded wire and then the other end of the strips of paper. Position the bead and strips of paper approx. 2in (5cm) down the wire. Secure the bead to the strips and wire with a blob of glue as in step 6.

8 Add another large bead to the wire and a small disc of paper measuring about ¾in (2cm) in diameter.

9 To make the tassel: from a page cut a rectangle of paper measuring 2 x 6in (5 x 15cm). Using scissors, cut a fringe all along the width of the paper, stopping ½in (1cm) from the other side (see illustration). Make the strips of the fringe about ¼in (5mm) wide. Run a glue stick along the top edge of the fringe and roll up to form the tassel. Glue a ½ x 2in (1 x 5cm) strip of paper around the top of the tassel for a neat finish.

10 Thread the tassel onto the wire. Use the small pair of pliers to bend the ends of wire over a few times to secure. Cut off any extra wire and hide the end of the wire among the tassels. Finally, open out the strips of paper to form a sphere. You can vary the shape of the decorations by changing the length of the strips of paper. You can also make double ones or even triple ones with different-sized spheres.

Spiky Decoration

Make this amazing decoration as a hanging feature or an object to display on a shelf. Wherever you place it, the intriguing spiny shape will always attract attention and, since it is made from the colorful pages of a brochure, this project is also a great way to recycle.

YOU WILL NEED
Pages from a brochure or magazine
Dinner plate to draw around
Plain paper
Pencil
Scissors
Needle
Ruler
Cutting mat
Craft knife
Glue
Strong thread
Card stock

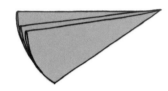

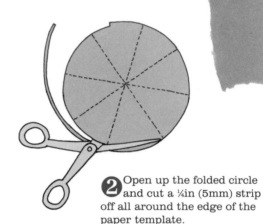

1 First make a plain paper template for the circles. Using a dinner plate as a guide, draw a circle on the plain piece of paper. My plate was 8in (20cm) in diameter, but you can make it any size. Cut out the circle, fold it in half, half again, and then half again.

2 Open up the folded circle and cut a ¼in (5mm) strip off all around the edge of the paper template.

3 Cut out ten circles from the magazine pages using the dinner plate to draw the circles. Lay the paper template on a circle so that there is a ¼in (5mm) gap between the outer edge of the template and the outer edge of the magazine circle. Make a mark in pencil at each fold line. Press the needle through the center point to mark the middle of the circle. Repeat for each of the ten circles.

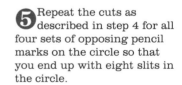

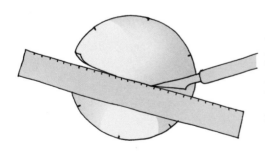

4 With a ruler, join two pencil marks opposite each other on the circle (one at the top and the opposite pencil mark at the bottom). Using the craft knife, cut along the ruler from the edge of the circle toward the center, stopping 1in (2.5cm) before the center point. Start to cut again 1in (2.5cm) on the other side of the center, taking the knife to the edge.

5 Repeat the cuts as described in step 4 for all four sets of opposing pencil marks on the circle so that you end up with eight slits in the circle.

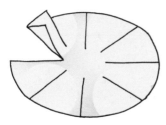

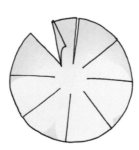

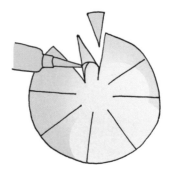

6 Take one of the segments and pinch it together to make a crease about 1in (2.5cm) along the center of the segment.

7 Lay the circle on the table with the creased segment to the left. Take the corner nearest to you on the creased segment and tuck it under, forming the paper into a cone shape. Try to make the edge of the cone shape line up with the centered crease. This may seem difficult at first but after a while it becomes easier, especially after you have done all 80 cones!

8 Hold the cone shape in position with your thumb and finger and cut off the other side of the segment in a triangle. Start the triangle 2in (5cm) down the slit that divides the segments. This should leave you with a ½in (1cm) strip of paper running parallel with the cone. Glue this strip and stick it around the cone.

9 Carry on moving clockwise around the circle making the cones. When you have completed one circle, move on to the next until you have finished all ten.

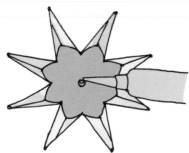

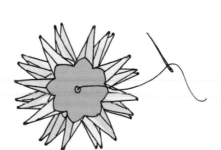

10 Cut out 20 small paper discs about ½in (1cm) in diameter. Stick on either side of every circle at the center point to strengthen this area.

11 Thread the needle with strong thread and make a large knot at the end. Thread through the center of each of the ten circles, from the front of the circles to the back. Pull the thread firmly, pushing the circles together and causing the pointed ends to form into a ball.

12 Cut a small disc of card stock, place a blob of glue on it, and pass it along the needle and thread to where the thread emerges from the back of the final circle. Secure the disc to the final circle. If you want to display the decoration standing on a shelf, you can trim off the spare thread.

Secret Hearts

YOU WILL NEED

Old book

Pencil

Tracing paper

Craft knife

Cutting mat

Scissors

While rummaging through a box of battered books at a local flea market I came across this little book, its pretty red cover embellished with gold lettering and embossed flowers. It grabbed my attention immediately, but when I opened the book to a chapter called "Hidden Treasure," I knew I had to buy the book and make a hidden, secret compartment within the pages.

1 Using the pencil and tracing paper, trace the heart from the template on page 121 and transfer it onto a page in your chosen book, a few pages in from the front. Center the heart on the page.

2 Start cutting out the heart-shaped cavity using the craft knife, saving the hearts as you cut each one out carefully (you need them to be whole). Cut down through the pages until you are nearly at the depth that you require. Slide the cutting mat between the pages at the level to which you want to cut, then finish off cutting the heart-shaped compartment.

3 To make the papercut hearts, either use the four different templates on page 121, or you can make up your own. If making your own pattern, fold each heart in half and, using a small pair of scissors, snip away a pattern through the two halves. Open it up to reveal the cut-out heart.

4 If you are using the templates, trace these and transfer the pattern onto the folded hearts before cutting out.

Oak Leaves and Acorns

You can achieve beautiful effects by using small amounts of silver leaf rubbed onto the pages of a book. I like the way the lettering is visible in between areas of silver. Wind them around some pretty ribbon to add vintage elegance to a specially wrapped gift.

YOU WILL NEED

Pages from books

Small amount of air-dry modeling clay

Glue and a glue stick

Silver leaf (I use the rub-down type attached to a backing sheet)

Scissors

Darning or large needle

Wire cutters

Thin craft wire

Small pliers

Pencil

Tracing paper

Craft knife

Cutting mat

1 To make the acorns: take a small amount of modeling clay and roll into an elongated ball, about the size of a marble or an acorn! Let it dry and then rub all over with the glue stick. Press the silver leaf down onto the tacky surface until the acorn is covered in silver.

2 Cut a strip of paper ¾in (2cm) wide and long enough to wrap around the acorn with at least ½in (1cm) to overlap. Wrap the strip of paper around the acorn, positioning it halfway down the acorn. Glue the overlap down to form a tube that overhangs the bottom of the acorn.

3 Pinch the overhanging bit of paper together to form a cup shape. Fold and press down the base so that the overlapping paper forms a flat base. You may find it easier to take the acorn out and place your finger in the cup. Glue the folded bits of paper down.

4 Make a hole in the middle of the base of the cup with the needle. Using wire cutters, cut a piece of wire approx. 3in (8cm) long. Use the pliers to bend the end of the wire over by a tiny amount and make a small knot at the end.

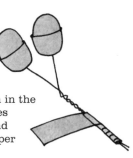

5 Thread the unturned end of the wire through the hole from the inside. Place the acorn back in the cup and glue it into position. Make another acorn in the same way, then twist the wires from both acorns together and wrap some glued strips of paper around to cover the wire.

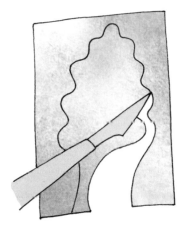

6 Using the pencil and tracing paper, trace the leaves from the template on page 121 and transfer these to some of the pages. Cut out the leaves using the craft knift and cutting mat.

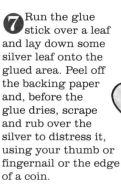

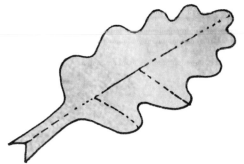

7 Run the glue stick over a leaf and lay down some silver leaf onto the glued area. Peel off the backing paper and, before the glue dries, scrape and rub over the silver to distress it, using your thumb or fingernail or the edge of a coin.

8 Fold the leaf in half lengthwise to make the main rib, sharpening the crease with your finger and thumb. Mark the veins of the leaf by making small creases from the center out to the center of each curved section of the leaf. Make more leaves in the same way.

9 Glue the ends of the leaves to the acorn stalk.

Watering Can

I am always on the lookout for old gardening books, especially those with hand-drawn pictures and diagrams. They depict a charming world of lovely old tools and neat wigwams of beans and sweetpeas. I did not want to cut these books up but they provide a great base to display this watering can and flowerpot.

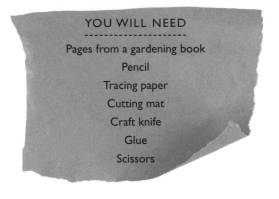

YOU WILL NEED

Pages from a gardening book
Pencil
Tracing paper
Cutting mat
Craft knife
Glue
Scissors

1 Using the pencil and tracing paper, trace the pieces for the watering can, flowerpot, and flower from the templates on page 121 and transfer these to one of the pages. Using scissors or the craft knife, cut out all the pieces. I have used black and white text for the watering can but used color for the flowerpot and flower. Mark in the glue flaps, as it is quite important to be precise on this project.

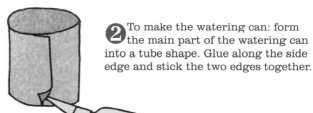

2 To make the watering can: form the main part of the watering can into a tube shape. Glue along the side edge and stick the two edges together.

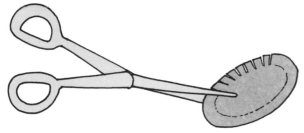

3 Make some snips all around the edge of the circular base of the watering can, being careful not to go over the marked line.

4 Fold up the snipped edge. Dot glue on the outside of the snipped flaps and insert the circular base into the bottom of the tube, sticking the flaps to the inside of the watering can.

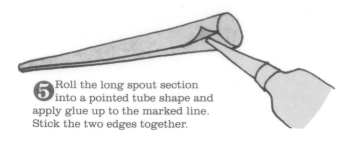

5 Roll the long spout section into a pointed tube shape and apply glue up to the marked line. Stick the two edges together.

6 Form the nozzle of the spout section into a cone shape and glue.

7 Make up the center of the nozzle section as you did the base of the watering can. Cut out the circle for the nozzle of the spout. Cut small slits all around the circle up to the edge of the glue flap marked on the template. Fold the flaps down to form a glue strip. Apply some glue and place inside the top of the nozzle.

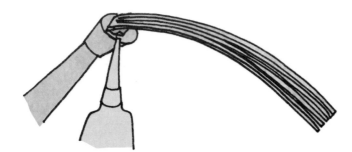

8 Cut a strip of paper ½ x 3½in (1cm x 9cm) and cut very thin ⅓₂in (1mm) slits all along the length, leaving ⅓in (1cm) uncut at the end. Glue this to the end of the top spout to make the cascade of water.

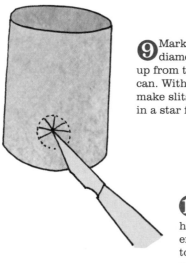

9 Mark a circle 15mm in diameter at ⅝in (1.5cm) up from the base of the can. With the craft knife make slits across the circle in a star formation.

10 Fold the triangle flaps to the inside of the can. Place a blob of glue onto the wide end of the water spout and push it into the hole, directing the end down to the base of the can. Hold this in position for a moment until the glue dries a bit.

11 Cut a strip of paper ¼ x 4⅓in (5mm x 11cm) for the top handle. Place a dab of glue on each end of the strip and stick the ends to the inside edge of the watering can, opposite each other to form a handle (see photograph on previous page for guidance).

12 Cut a strip measuring ¼ x 3½in (5mm x 9cm) and fold in each end by ¼in (5mm). Curve the paper into a side handle shape and stick each end to the side of the watering can, positioning it opposite the spout.

13 To make the flowerpot: cut out the pot section using the template on page 121. Form the pot section into a tube shape and glue the edges together as you did for the main part of the watering can.

14 Use the template on page 121 to cut out a circle for the soil. Cut a small slit ¼in (5mm) wide in the center of the soil. Use the remaining template to cut out the flower from a colored piece of paper. Insert the stalk of the flower into the slit in the center of the soil. Place the circle of soil into the top of the flowerpot. You shouldn't need any glue here as the circle will fit snugly into the pot a short way down from the top edge.

For Kids

Vintage Papier-Mâché Dolls

These elegant paper ladies are probably the most challenging of all the projects, but well worth the effort. Use book pages for the body and try to seek out pretty floral pictures for the clothes. Music score sheets are good for the skirts. Keep a look out for the vintage ones with decoration and wonderfully ornate lettering. These dolls do take time to complete but each lady will be unique and something to treasure always.

YOU WILL NEED

Pages from books

Modeling clay

Tracing paper

Plastic wrap or cling film

Wallpaper paste and paintbrush

Mixing bowl

Craft knife

Cutting mat

Quick-drying, strong glue

Pencil

Large needle

Round elastic

Quilling tool

White and pink paint

Black pen

1 Using modeling clay and the templates on page 122 as a guide, mold shapes for the body section, two arms, and two legs. Leave the clay to dry. When the clay is hard, wrap each part in a small piece of plastic wrap. Try to get it smooth and don't allow it to bunch up.

2 Tear up some book pages into small squares no bigger than ½–¾in (1–2cm) in length. Mix up a small amount of wallpaper paste at the bottom of the mixing bowl. Place some pieces of paper around the bowl and brush them with paste. This way you can do a few at a time and it contains the mess a little! Repeat until all the body sections are covered with three or four layers of paper and leave to dry.

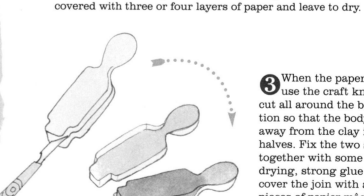

3 When the paper is dry, use the craft knife to cut all around the body section so that the body comes away from the clay in two halves. Fix the two sections together with some quick-drying, strong glue and cover the join with a few pieces of papier mâché. Repeat for the arms and legs. Leave to dry.

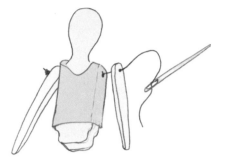

④ To make the lady's top: cut a strip of paper that will wrap around the body with a bit extra for gluing. Mark the center at the neck in pencil and cut a small semicircle here for the neckline. Place a few blobs of glue on the back of the paper and position it around the doll, making sure that the neckline is positioned in the center.

⑤ To attach the arms to the body, thread a large needle with a piece of round elastic knotted at one end. Make a hole with a long sharp needle through the center top of the arm, approx. ½in (1cm) from the top. Thread the elastic through the arm, continue through the top of the body, and out the other side. Take the elastic through the other arm in the same way. Make a knot in the elastic where it emerges from the arm and trim off any spare elastic. Use the same method to attach the legs to the body.

⑥ To make the skirt: cut a piece of paper that goes three times around the body and reaches from the waist to mid-calf. Make pleats along the top edge of the paper until it fits snugly around the body with approx. ⅓in (8mm) left as an overlap. When you are satisfied that the waist is the right measurement, put a blob of glue at the top of each pleat to hold it in position. Place the skirt around the body and glue down the edge of the skirt to the back of the body. Stick the other edge of the skirt to this, making sure that the skirt fits snugly around the waist.

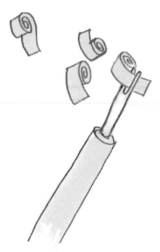

⑦ For the hair: take small strips of paper approx. ¼in (5mm) wide, and use the quilling tool to make curls. Follow the instructions on using a quilling tool in the Whirlygig Brooch project (see page 84).

⑧ To make the face: use watered-down white paint to paint an oval on the head section, then draw in black eyes and nose, and a rosy mouth and cheeks. Stick the curls from step 7 flat to the head as shown on the smaller doll, or place a blob of glue on the flat tab of paper at the end of the curl and attach that to the head. This will give the appearance of looser curls. You could use a combination of both methods and invent some very ornate hairdos! Follow the instructions in the Pop-up Flowers Book project (page 46) to make some flowers to place in the hair or on the waist.

Jumping Jacks

Dust jackets on old books often get very tattered but the designs can be wonderful, with repeat patterns in gorgeous colors. Transform odd scraps into these delightfully old-fashioned Jumping Jacks—pull the string to make them jump. A row of these dancing Cossacks would make a quirky display.

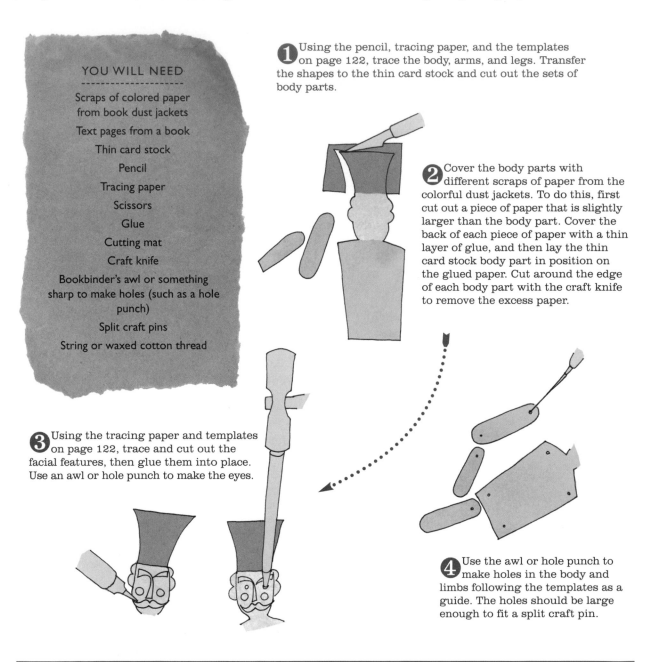

YOU WILL NEED

Scraps of colored paper from book dust jackets

Text pages from a book

Thin card stock

Pencil

Tracing paper

Scissors

Glue

Cutting mat

Craft knife

Bookbinder's awl or something sharp to make holes (such as a hole punch)

Split craft pins

String or waxed cotton thread

1 Using the pencil, tracing paper, and the templates on page 122, trace the body, arms, and legs. Transfer the shapes to the thin card stock and cut out the sets of body parts.

2 Cover the body parts with different scraps of paper from the colorful dust jackets. To do this, first cut out a piece of paper that is slightly larger than the body part. Cover the back of each piece of paper with a thin layer of glue, and then lay the thin card stock body part in position on the glued paper. Cut around the edge of each body part with the craft knife to remove the excess paper.

3 Using the tracing paper and templates on page 122, trace and cut out the facial features, then glue them into place. Use an awl or hole punch to make the eyes.

4 Use the awl or hole punch to make holes in the body and limbs following the templates as a guide. The holes should be large enough to fit a split craft pin.

5 Make another slightly smaller hole between the first hole and the top edge of both upper arms and upper legs. (You will be threading the string through these.)

6 Join all the pieces together with the split craft pins, making sure that the arms and legs can move freely. Cover the boots and glove pieces with colorful paper and stick them in position.

7 Thread a piece of string or thread, approx. 4¾in (12cm) long, through one hole at the top of the arm and up through the hole on the other arm. If you find this difficult to do with the arms clipped in position, slip them out of the split craft pins and then reposition.

8 Tie the two ends of string or thread together so that a loop is formed between the two arms. The loop should be neither too loose nor too tight. Tie it with the arms in a down position and test to see that if you pull the loop in the middle, pinching both bits of string, the arms will move up.

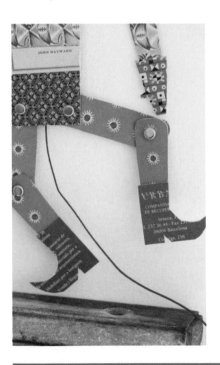

9 Do the same for the legs (repeat steps 7 and 8). Then take a piece of string approx. 12in (30cm) long and tie it first around the top loop centered between the two arms and then around the loop between the two legs. You may need to adjust the strings to get the tension right.

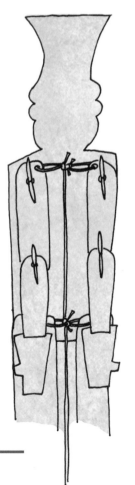

Whirlygig Brooch

Made by simply winding thin strips of paper very tightly, these brooches are like mini sculptures. The elegant curls around the edge that surrounds the surprisingly robust central disc and the soft, subtle colors make these very wearable.

YOU WILL NEED

Pages from a book

Craft knife

Ruler

Cutting mat

Quick-drying, strong glue and a glue stick

Quilling tool

Brooch pin

1 Using the craft knife, ruler, and cutting mat cut some strips of paper ½in (1cm) wide from the page of a book. Fold each strip in half so that the strips are ¼in (5mm) wide.

2 Take one of the folded strips and start to roll it up. Try to get the first bit quite tight so that you don't have a gap in the middle. As you roll it up, run a glue stick along the back of the strip. It doesn't matter if the glue does not cover the whole strip. Continue rolling until the strip is completely rolled.

3 Place a dab of glue on the end of the next strip and continue adding on strip by strip until you have a disc the size you would like. Mine measures about 1in (2.5cm) across. Make sure that you keep the folded side of the strip facing upward as you add the strips.

4 Use the quilling tool to make some curls. Take a strip of the folded paper and place the end into the top of the quilling tool. Start winding the paper around the tip of the tool, keeping it quite tight.

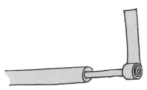

5 When you have finished winding, let the strip of paper go so that it springs loose, and remove it gently from the tool. Experiment to get the right length and tightness of curl. You can try to get them all the same size or vary them—both look good.

6 Place a blob of quick-drying glue on the flat tab of paper at the end of the curl. This tab should be no longer than ⅛in (1cm); if it is longer, snip it off. Stick the curl to your disc. Continue sticking curls around the disc, making sure that each curl touches the next.

7 Place some strong glue onto a brooch pin and secure in position on to the back of the brooch. To make your brooch more durable you could give it a coat of matte varnish. I find that although they look very delicate, the brooches are actually quite sturdy.

Stand-up Lion

This cheerful creature is a greeting card and a decoration for a child's bedroom all rolled into one. I have used brightly colored pages from a children's picture book and mixed in some lovely curly script lettering for the mane.

YOU WILL NEED

Pages from children's books

Letter-sized piece of
thin card stock

Glue and a glue stick

Pencil

Tracing paper

Scissors

Craft knife

Cutting mat

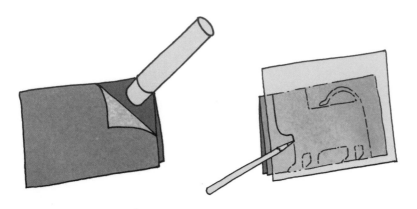

1 Fold the letter-sized piece of thin card in half. Stick a piece of brightly colored paper from a children's book to one half of the card.

2 Using the pencil and tracing paper, trace the lion body, head, and face features from the templates on page 123 and transfer these onto the card.

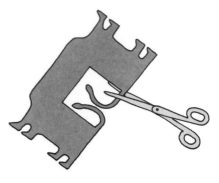

3 Cut out the body shape through both layers of card using scissors (or a craft knife and cutting mat for tricky bits). Cut off the tail on the back non-colored section of the card, as this is not really needed.

4 Using the craft knife on the cutting mat, cut out the face, features, and strips of paper, ¼in (5mm) wide and 1½in (4cm) long, for the mane.

5 Glue the strips all around the outside of the face to make the mane.

6 Stick the nose, eyes, and whiskers into position on the face. Glue the head onto the body to finish.

Take-out Noodles and Shrimp

You can make anything out of paper, even a Chinese take-out! It looks complicated to make but is, in fact, very easy. Look out for some pink paper for the shrimps—I used a section from an old children's encyclopedia. I found the word "shrimp" in the contents and have used it for the antennae.

1 To make the carton: using the pencil and tracing paper, trace the carton from the template on page 123 and transfer it onto some thin card stock; transfer all the dotted scoring lines. Cut out the shape using the craft knife and cutting mat.

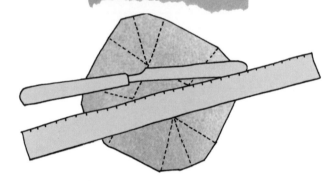

2 Score all the lines marked on the templates using the ruler and blunt knife (see page 117 for more detailed instructions on scoring card and paper).

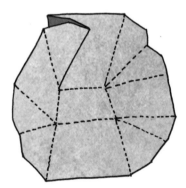

3 Crease the score lines at the corner of the carton into a triangle shape, pushing it inward to form the sides of the carton. Repeat on the other three corners until all the four sides are formed.

4 Using the awl or darning needle, make a hole at the center of the overlapping section, positioning it about ¼in (5mm) down from the top edge and making sure that it goes through the two overlapping triangles. Make a hole on the other side in the same position.

5 Make the carton handle by using the wire cutters to cut a length of thin wire measuring 6in (15cm). Push the wire through the lined-up holes on one side of the carton. Using the small pliers, bend back ½in (1cm) of wire inside the carton to hold the wire in place. Thread the other end of the wire through the hole on the other side of the carton and bend in place to secure.

6 To make the noodles: cut thin strips of paper ¹⁄₁₆in (2mm) wide. Wind them around your fingers and scrunch them up a bit to form the noodles. Place these inside the carton.

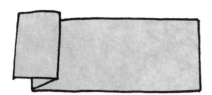

7 To make the shrimp: cut out a piece of pink paper measuring 4¾ x 1¾in (12 x 4.5cm). Starting ¾in (2cm) down from the end of the rectangle, make a concertina fold of about ¼in (5mm).

8 Make four more folds evenly spaced along the strip, leaving ½in (1cm) unfolded at the end. Fold the rectangle in half lengthwise.

9 With the folded rectangle, cut out a shape similar to a half-fish shape.

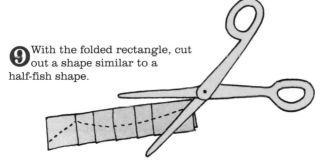

10 Gently ease out the folds to give the shrimp a nicely curved and realistic shape.

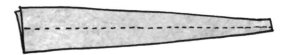

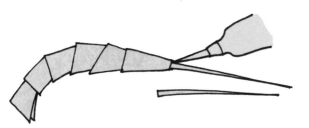

11 Cut two thin strips of paper measuring 2¼in (5.5cm) long and ¹⁄₁₆in (2mm) wide, tapering to ¹⁄₃₂in (1mm). Stick these to the inside of the head section. Make another shrimp in the same way.

12 To make the chopsticks: cut out a tapered piece of paper measuring 6¼in (16cm) long and 2¼in (5.5cm) wide at one end and 1¼in (3cm) wide at the other end. Glue the strip and fold it in half. Glue the strip again and fold in half again. Make two chopsticks.

13 Stick one of the shrimp between the ends of the chopsticks.

FOR KIDS ✳

Folk-inspired Papercuts

A few simple snips with some scissors can transform an ordinary scrap of paper into a beautiful work of art. It is always a pleasure and a surprise to unfold the paper and reveal the intricate, delicate pattern. Glue your pretty papercuts to plain colored paper for gorgeous gift wrap or cards, or group them together in a frame on a colored background for an original piece of art.

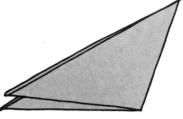

YOU WILL NEED

Pages from a book

Card stock or colored paper

Pencil

Tracing paper

Small pair of scissors or a craft knife and cutting mat

Glue

1 Take a piece of paper from the pages of the book measuring 4¾in (12cm) square.

2 Fold the square in half to make a triangle, and then fold in half again.

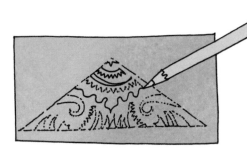

3 Using the pencil and tracing paper, trace the pattern from the template on page 124 and transfer it to the triangle.

4 Cut away the pattern using the small pair of scissors or the craft knife, and open up the cut triangle to reveal all. At this point you can glue your papercut to card stock or to paper to make a greeting card, gift wrap, or a piece of artwork.

Animals

Wise Owl

This little owl is happy perched in his home nestled among the pages of a book. You will need to find an old cloth-bound book so that you can cut away the cardboard to reveal the branches and leaves he perches on.

YOU WILL NEED

Cloth-bound book, approx. 5 x 8in (12.5 x 20cm)

Some scraps of colored paper taken from a book

Thin card

Pencil

Tracing paper

Craft knife

Cutting mat

Glue stick

1 Using the pencil, tracing paper, and template on page 124, trace the owl, moon, branch, and hole shapes. Put the owl template to one side and, using the pencil, transfer the other shapes onto the front of the book. You may have to adjust the trace to fit your book if it is a very different shape. With the craft knife, cut around the design on the front, cutting through the cloth layer to reveal the brown cardboard underneath. Cut through the cover and approx. halfway through the pages of the book to create the hole.

2 To make the owl, stick a page from the book onto some thin card or, alternatively, stick two or three pages together. Using the owl template and the pencil, transfer the owl shape onto the paper and cut around it.

3 To make some feathers, cut small V-shaped slits into the lower half of the owl and pull them forward.

4 Using the templates on page 124, trace the eyes, forehead, and beak onto tracing paper, then transfer the shapes onto some colored pages, cut them out, and stick in position on the owl's body.

5 Stick the owl into position in the hole shape, gluing the base to the inside cover of the book.

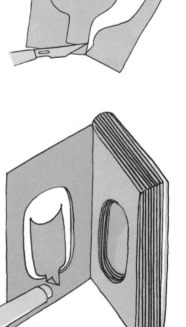

Butterflies

Transform a worn-out children's book into these lovely creatures instead of consigning it to the recycling bin. The pretty butterflies emerge from the colorful pages to brighten up a dull corner—or string them up to make a vibrant, eye-catching mobile.

1 To make the wings: using colorful pages, cut two pieces of paper, each measuring 4¾ x 6¼in (12 x16cm). Take one of the pieces and fold down a ½in (1cm) strip along the longest side of the paper. Fold another ½in- (1cm-) deep strip back the other way to make a pleated zig zag. Continue to fold over ½in- (1cm-) deep strips until you reach the end and have what looks like a fan or concertina. Repeat this folding with the other piece of paper, but this time folding it along its shortest side.

2 Open out the concertina shape at one of the corners and cut the corner off in a rounded, curved shape. Repeat this with all the corners on both concertina pieces.

3 To make the body: cut out a rectangle of colorful paper from the book measuring 1 x 5¼in (2.5 x 13.5cm) Glue this rectangle to a piece of card stock of the same size using the glue stick.

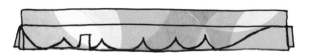

4 Fold the rectangle in half lengthwise with the color on the outside. Using the pencil and tracing paper, trace the body shape from the template on page 125 and transfer this onto half of the folded rectangle.

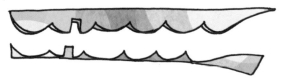

5 Cut out the butterfly body shape with scissors and make the slot for the wings with the craft knife. You may have to adjust the size of the slot. If your paper is very thick, then make the slot a little wider.

ANIMALS ✳

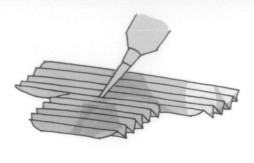

6 Take the larger concertina piece (large wing) and place a dab of glue on the outer folded strip at the center. Stick the larger wing to the smaller concertina piece (small wing), matching the two centers.

7 Pinch the two wings together at the center and place a blob of glue on the top and sides at this point. Thread the folded wings into the slot made in the body and unfurl the wings once they are in place. Add a bit of glue where the wings join the body.

8 To make the antennae: cut two strips of paper ¼in (5mm) wide and 6in (15cm) long. Use the quilling pen or wrap around your pencil to make the curl in the antennae, then glue the ends to the underside of the head section.

Three Little Mice

I found an interior design brochure with a bright yellow inside cover that was perfect for a block of Cheddar cheese! If you can't find something suitable, use some yellow card stock instead.

YOU WILL NEED

Text pages from a book
Thin yellow card
Pencil
Tracing paper
Cutting mat
Craft knife
Glue
Black pen

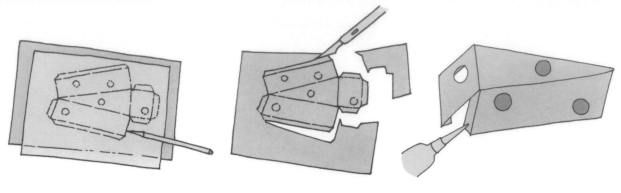

1 To make the cheese: using the pencil and tracing paper, trace the cheese template on page 125 and transfer the template onto some thin yellow card.

2 Using the cutting mat and craft knife, cut out the cheese shape. Cut out the holes in the cheese. Score the fold lines that are marked on the template and fold to make the cheese block shape (see the Cutout Greeting Cards project on page 12 for how to score fold lines).

3 Place some glue on the three glue flaps and stick into position, tucking them to the inside of the cheese.

4 To make the mice: using the pencil and tracing paper, trace the mouse template on page 125, and transfer onto a piece of paper from the book. Lightly mark the fold lines on the mouse. Cut out the shape.

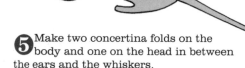

5 Make two concertina folds on the body and one on the head in between the ears and the whiskers.

6 Fold the mouse in half lengthwise. Fold up the ears and pinch them gently between your thumb and finger to make a crease down the center of each ear.

7 Cut the two whisker sections into 4 strips each. The strips should get narrower as they get nearer the head. Curl the ends of the whiskers around a pencil and do the same with the tail to make a nice curly tail.

8 Draw on two eyes with the black pen (see photograph for guidance).

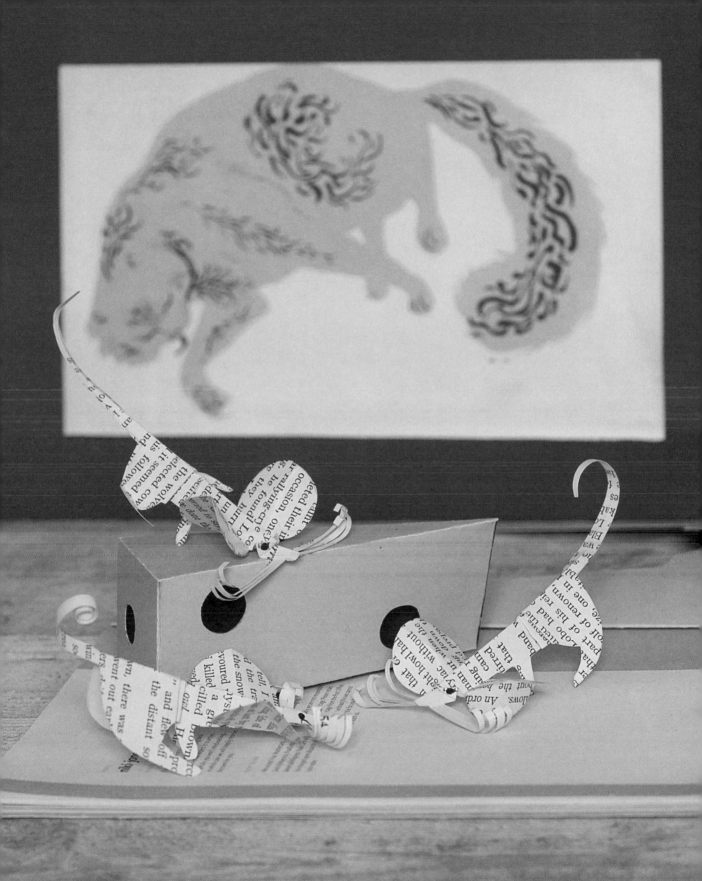

Robin and Nest

There is a little robin that visits my garden. Looking up from my work I sometimes see him hopping about and it is always such a cheery sight. I knew I wanted to make a paper robin and surprised myself at how much character I was able to achieve. This may well be one of my favorite projects in the book.

YOU WILL NEED

Pages from old books, including some red, brown, and blue scraps from illustrations

Thin wire
(florists' or craft wire)

Wire cutters or scissors

Small pair of pliers

Glue

White paper

Black pen

Cardboard egg carton

Small pebble

1 Wind some wire to form a ball roughly the size of a plum. Cut off the end of the wire with the wire cutters or scissors and stick the end into the ball. Pinch the wire into a head shape and round body. Pull out a folded double bit of wire for the beak.

2 Thread another piece of wire through the body section at the end of the ball and bend the two ends around to form it into a tail shape about 1in (2.5cm) long. Wind the wire back across the tail shape a couple of times for strength. Cut any spare wire and hide the end within the body.

3 To make the feet: take a piece of wire approx. 20in (50cm) long. At about 6¼in (16cm) along the length of wire from the left, fold the wire back so that it becomes double. With the pliers, pinch about ⅜in (1cm) and twist it around to make one toe. Next to this toe form the wire into a loop ⅜in (1cm) in length and twist this around with the pliers to form the second toe. Repeat for the third toe and then twist the spare wire around the leg for about 1in (2.5cm).

4 Thread the end of the wire without the foot through the wire-ball body from the underside and about two-thirds along the length of the body. Bend the wire as it emerges at the top of the body and reinsert it to bring it out with a ⅜in (1cm) gap between the two legs. Create three more toes on this bit of wire, matching up the lengths to the first leg and toes. Wind the spare wire around the leg until it reaches the body. Cut off any excess and hide the end in the body.

5 From some pale-colored pages, tear out small pieces of paper about ⅜in (1cm) square, and start gluing these down onto the wire shape. Overlap the pieces, leaving bare the feet and two-thirds of the wire tail. Do two layers of pale-colored pieces.

6 Tear up some very small pieces of red paper, no bigger than ⅜ x ¼in (10 x 5mm), and glue these overlapping each other on the robin's breast and throat. Use small pieces of brown paper of the same size over the top of the head and the back.

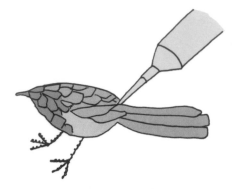

7 Tear out some slightly larger, longer brown pieces for the wings on either side of the body, and some even longer strips to cover the length of the wire tail. Glue these in position.

8 On some white paper, draw up two eyes in black ink, leaving the center of the eye white. Cut out the eyes and stick them in position with a dot of glue.

9 To make the nest: cut one compartment from a cardboard egg carton. Cut some paper from a text page into roughly ¹⁄₁₆in (2mm) strips. Paste some glue on the egg compartment and wind some strips of paper around. Build up some layers by adding more glue and paper. Try not to wind in the same direction all the time and make some areas looser than others for a more natural look.

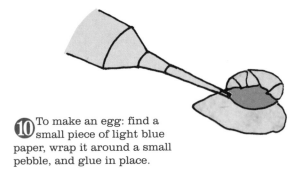

10 To make an egg: find a small piece of light blue paper, wrap it around a small pebble, and glue in place.

Birds in Flight

I recently found an old atlas; its cover was missing but I could see immediately that the pages would be lovely to work with. The paper was thick, and the colors very soft; just the kind of look I wanted for these graceful birds.

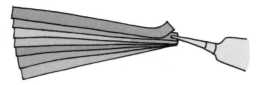

1 To make the body: cut seven strips of paper from the atlas measuring 10 x 1in (25 x 2.5cm). Place the strips flat on the table, overlapping the ends so that the strips fan out, but are still overlapping. Put a dab of glue in between each strip at the top to stick them together.

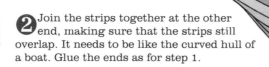

2 Join the strips together at the other end, making sure that the strips still overlap. It needs to be like the curved hull of a boat. Glue the ends as for step 1.

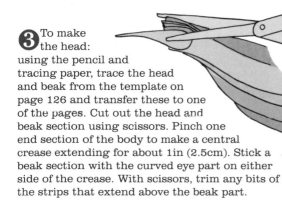

3 To make the head: using the pencil and tracing paper, trace the head and beak from the template on page 126 and transfer these to one of the pages. Cut out the head and beak section using scissors. Pinch one end section of the body to make a central crease extending for about 1in (2.5cm). Stick a beak section with the curved eye part on either side of the crease. With scissors, trim any bits of the strips that extend above the beak part.

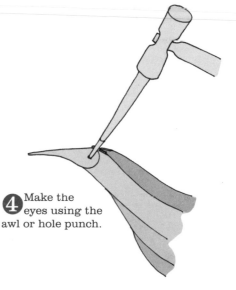

4 Make the eyes using the awl or hole punch.

5 To make the wings and tail: trace the wings and tail from the templates on page 126 and transfer these to one of the pages. Cut out the two wings; using the template for guidance, cut out the scalloped pattern on the wings with the craft knife. Using the ruler and the back of the blunt knife, score along the top of the scallops and fold each scallop out.

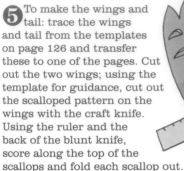

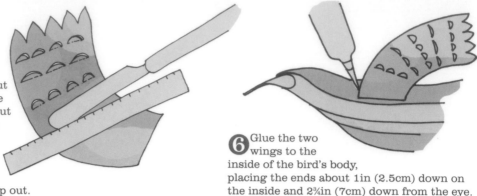

6 Glue the two wings to the inside of the bird's body, placing the ends about 1in (2.5cm) down on the inside and 2¾in (7cm) down from the eye.

7 Trim the strips of paper at the tail end to make a neat end. Cut out the tail section and glue it in position.

8 To cover the wooden skewer: follow the instructions in the Owl and the Pussycat Pop-up project on page 110.

9 To cover the block of wood: place the block on a page taken from a book. Draw around the base. Take the block away and with a ruler extend the lines of the block out to make four flaps that are ½in (1cm) longer than the depth of your block of wood.

10 Cut out the paper for the box on the cutting mat using the ruler and craft knife. Brush some glue over the paper, place the block back into its position, and stick the flaps over the sides, turning the ½in (1cm) extra under the wood for a neat finish.

11 Cut two rectangles of map paper, each measuring 4¾ x 1½in (12 x 4cm). Stick these together for strength. Score two lines across the width of the strip, about ¾in (2cm) in from each end. Fold the flaps back to 90 degrees and stick the flaps to each side of the inner body of the bird about 4⅜in (11cm) down from the eye. Line up the bend of the paper to the top edge of the bird's body. This acts as a bridge between the two sides of the bird and gives the bird strength, whether you position it on the skewer or attach string to it here, if you want to hang the bird up.

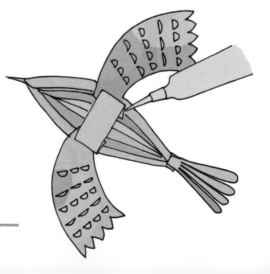

12 If mounting the bird on a skewer, then drill a hole in the block of wood to the width of the paper-covered skewer. Make a hole of the same size in the underside body of the bird about 3¾in (9.5cm) up from the end of the body where the tail begins. Place the skewer into the block and through the hole in the bird. Place some quick-drying strong glue on the end of the skewer and stick it to the underside of the support bridge across the bird. Hold it in position for a moment or two until it dries.

Owl and the Pussycat Pop-up

Edward Lear's poem 'The Owl and the Pussycat' has delighted people for over 140 years. Since it was written, many illustrators and designers have depicted the pair in their boat, the first of whom was Lear himself with a wonderful pen-and-ink drawing. I did wonder if I should bring color to my version, but decided I liked the old-fashioned charm of the black print and soft cream paper.

Note: I have cut some waves directly from the pages of the book and others I have cut separately and stuck in. The instructions below are for waves that are cut from separate sheets and glued into the book. See the Pop-up Flowers Book project on page 46 for a detailed description of how to cut images straight into a page within a book.

YOU WILL NEED

Book with some pages removed to cut up

Pencil

Tracing paper

Craft knife

Cutting mat

Glue and a glue stick

Scissors

Wooden barbecue skewer

Bookbinder's awl or compass

Quilling tool

Small piece of black paper

1 To make the waves: using the pencil and tracing paper, trace the three wave images from the templates on page 126 and transfer these to one of the pages you have removed from the book. Using the craft knife, cut out a selection of waves in the three different sizes. Once you have cut out a number of waves, lightly score each wave; place the tip of the craft knife at the center base of the wave to the right of the glue flap. Draw the blade gently around the curve, keeping to the center of the wave right around to the tip of the wave. Keep an even pressure but don't press too hard. You need to just break the surface of the paper, not go all the way through.

2 Gently pinch along the scored line with your finger and thumb while easing the end of the wave in a circular motion toward the middle. This does get easier with practice!

3 Place the open book on the table. Fold back the glue flap at the base of a wave, apply some glue, and stick it to the front page nearest to you. Arrange the waves with larger ones toward the back and smaller ones toward the front. Glue them pointing in both directions. Leave a space of at least 2½in (6cm) between the last row of waves and the spine. Stick some waves on the opposite page to appear behind the boat.

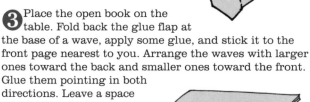

4 To make the boat: using the pencil and tracing paper, trace the boat, sail, flag, and moon from the templates on page 126, and transfer these to one or two loose pages. Cut out the boat shape with the craft knife or scissors. Fold back the glue flap, apply glue, and stick the boat to the book just behind the waves on the first page.

5 Make the mast using a wooden skewer: break it to measure 6¾in (17cm) in length. From a page of the book, cut a rectangle of paper the same length as the stick and approx. ½in (1cm) wide. Lay the rectangle on the table, run the glue stick along it, place the stick along the edge, and roll the paper around the stick.

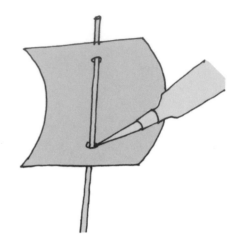

6 Cut out the sail. Make two small holes with the awl or compass point about ⅝in (1.5cm) up from the center top and bottom edge. Thread the sail onto the stick. Place a blob of glue at the bottom of the sail to secure it to the covered stick. Do the same with the top of the sail, pushing the sail down the stick a bit so that it curves out. Leave approx. 1½in (4cm) at the top for the flag.

7 Cut out the flag and the moon. Put glue on the flap of the flag and wrap it around the top of the mast. Place a blob of glue at the bottom of the crescent moon shape and stick it to the corner of the sail.

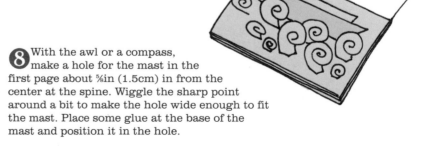

8 With the awl or a compass, make a hole for the mast in the first page about ⅝in (1.5cm) in from the center at the spine. Wiggle the sharp point around a bit to make the hole wide enough to fit the mast. Place some glue at the base of the mast and position it in the hole.

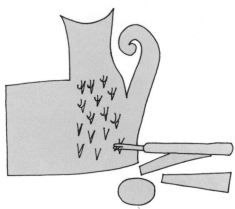

9 To make the cat templates: using the pencil and tracing paper, trace the various parts of the cat from the templates on page 126, and transfer all of these to one or two of the pages. Cut out the cat's body, face, and whisker sections from the text page. Make thin triangular cuts all over the front of the body up to the head. Push these forward and curl slightly with the quilling tool.

10 Transfer the features of the cat's face from the template onto the oval face section and cut out with a craft knife. Stick a piece of black paper behind the nose and mouth and two small pieces behind the eye slits.

11 Take the whisker section and cut four even strips along the length, stopping ½in (1cm) from the thinner end. Curl the whiskers with the quilling tool and glue in position to the back of the face. Repeat on the other side of the face. Stick the face and whiskers to the head section of the main piece.

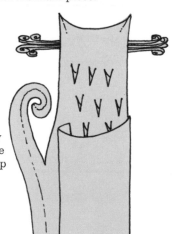

12 To curl the tail: use the same method of scoring and pinching as you did for the waves.

13 Curve the body around to make a tube. Glue the flap and stick it down.

14 The owl is made in the same way as the cat. Follow the cut and score lines on the template to cut out the wings, beak, and feathers (and use the photographs as a guide). When the cat and owl are complete, stand both figures up behind the boat.

Wooly Sheep

I always keep a box of old magazines for art projects, and among them was a lovely black-and-white photograph of a wooly sheep, the inspiration for this project. I used the photograph as the background but you could use anything you like—green rolling hills and fields would work really well.

YOU WILL NEED

Picture from a
magazine or book

Thin white card stock

Glue

Pencil

Tracing paper

Craft knife

Cutting mat

Quilling tool

Blunt knife

Ruler

Hole punch

1 If your background picture is on thin paper, you will need to stick it to some thin white card stock for added strength.

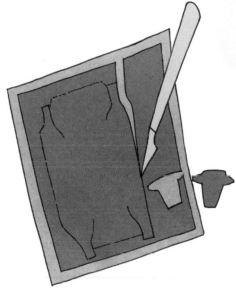

2 Using the pencil and tracing paper, trace the sheep body and face from the template on page 126 and transfer these to the card onto which you have glued your picture. Cut these out using the craft knife and mat.

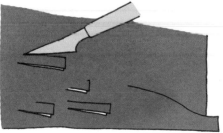

3 Make slits in the body. Several examples are drawn on the template but you don't have to follow this precisely since a bit of variation in size and number is a good thing. Note that the top edge of each slit is left uncut on both sides, so, once you have completed the first side, turn the paper around so that the other side of the sheep is facing you and repeat cutting the slits on this side. This way the curls will curl upward.

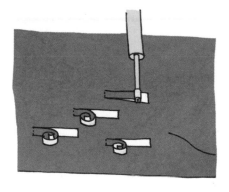

4 Use the quilling tool to make a curl out of each of the slits (see the Whirlygig Brooches project on page 84 for instructions on how to use a quilling tool).

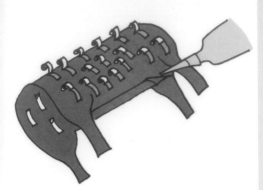

5 Bend the body around into a tube shape and, at the same time, straighten the legs out into a standing position. Apply glue to the flap on one edge of the body section and stick it to the other side to make the tube-shaped body.

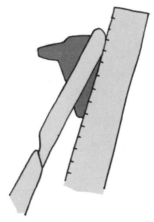

6 Using the back of the blunt knife and the ruler, score the lines marked on the head template and crease to make the face into a 3-D shape.

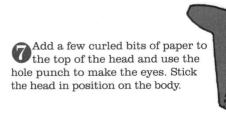

7 Add a few curled bits of paper to the top of the head and use the hole punch to make the eyes. Stick the head in position on the body.

8 To make some grass, cut a rectangle of paper from a magazine. Cut triangle-shaped slits all over the page and fold them up from the page at right angles.

TOOLS & MATERIALS

ESSENTIAL TOOLS

Scissors, small and large

Scalpel or craft knife

Cutting mat

Metal ruler

Bookbinder's awl

Hole punch, with different
size heads

Hammer to use with
the hole punch

Triangle (set square)

Pencils, hard 4 (2H) and
softer 2 (HB)

Eraser

Something for scoring (blunt knife)

Compass

Quilling tool

Small pliers/wire cutters

USEFUL BUT NOT ESSENTIAL

Bone folder for making
sharp creases

A soft brush to sweep away
bits of eraser

ADHESIVES

I use different types of glue for different
projects and I also use different
adhesive tapes. With glue sticks, try to
find one with clear glue because this
type never seems to clog up. Wood
(PVA) glue is white when it goes on but
dries clear and is a very good adhesive
for large areas. Use a brush or a small
piece of card stock to apply it. Strong,
quick-drying glue is clear and usually
comes in a tube. You will also need
several types of adhesive tape, for
instance: masking tape, double-sided
tape, and clear tape.

USEFUL TIPS

These tips are useful techniques that will
either save you time or help to give your
projects a more professional look.

Enlarging templates
Some of the templates on pages 118–126
will need to be enlarged and the easiest
way to do this is on a photocopier—the
percentage enlargement you will need is
given. A few projects may not fit on a
tabloid size (A3) page. For these, the
templates will have to be enlarged in
sections and joined together with tape.

Tracing
For many projects you need to transfer
the template onto paper or card stock,
using tracing paper. Place a sheet of
tracing paper over the template and
secure with some masking tape. Trace
the lines with a hard 4 (2H) pencil, then
turn the tracing paper over and go over
the lines again on the reverse with a
softer pencil, such as a 2 (HB). Now turn
the tracing paper over again and place it
in position on your chosen paper or
card stock. Go over all the lines carefully
with the 4 (2H) pencil, and then remove
the tracing paper. This will give you a
nice, clear outline.

Cutting
I use a scalpel or craft knife for nearly all
my projects. Make sure the blade is sharp
and that you always use a cutting mat.
When you need to make a straight cut,
use a metal ruler and keep the blade in
contact with the ruler at all times. Cut
toward you, keeping an even pressure.

Scoring
It is important to score before making
any fold. If it helps, you can draw a
pencil line first to help you score in the
right place. Place a metal ruler along the
line and then score down the line, using
the back, blunt edge of a craft knife or the
blunt side of a cutlery knife. Make sure
you keep the side of the blade in
contact with the ruler.

Folding
Line up your edges carefully. Fold away
from you, creasing down with the palm
of your hand. Use a bone folder if you
want an extra sharp crease.

Quilling
Put the tip of the strip of paper in the slot
of your quilling tool, making sure it's at a
right angle to the tool. Hold on to the
end of the strip with one hand and with
the other roll the tool away from you,
making sure you roll in a straight line so
that the coil is evenly aligned. If you
require a tight coil, use a dab of glue to fix
the end in place, or if you want a looser
coil simply let the paper uncoil itself.

Templates

Birdcage Cards (page 10)
Enlarge to twice this size

Cage 1

Cage 2

Cage 3

Rabbit

Cut-out Greetings Cards (page 12)
Enlarge to twice this size

Fish

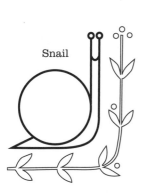

Snail

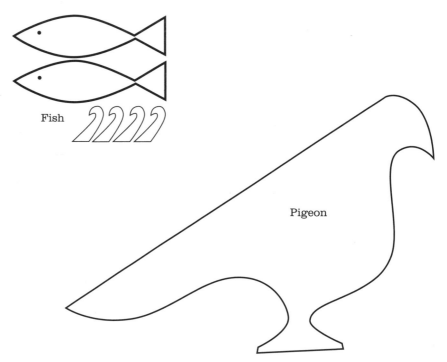

Pigeon

Bird

Nest

Little Bird Prints (page 15)
Actual size

Pigeon Message Card (page 22)
Actual size

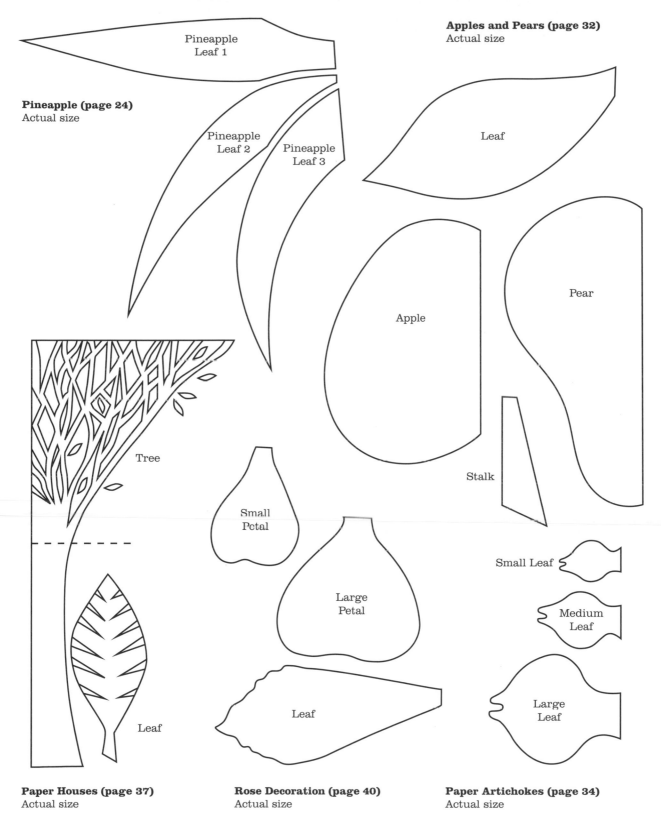

Pineapple (page 24)
Actual size

Pineapple
Leaf 1

Pineapple
Leaf 2

Pineapple
Leaf 3

Apples and Pears (page 32)
Actual size

Leaf

Apple

Pear

Stalk

Tree

Small Leaf

Medium
Leaf

Small
Petal

Large
Petal

Large
Leaf

Leaf

Leaf

Paper Houses (page 37)
Actual size

Rose Decoration (page 40)
Actual size

Paper Artichokes (page 34)
Actual size

119

Sculptural Shapes (page 42)
Enlarge to twice this size

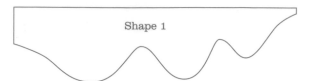

Shape 1

Shape 2

Shape 4

Shape 3

Winter Village Scene (page 44)
Enlarge to twice this size

Row of Houses

Row of Trees

Flower
Shape

Pop-up Flowers Book (page 46)
Actual size

Abstract
Shape 1

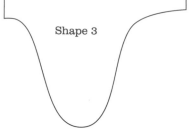

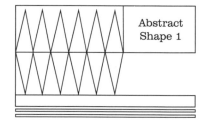

Abstract
Shape 2

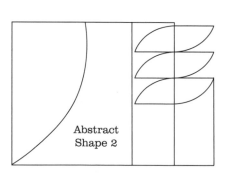

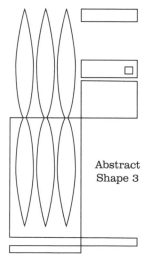

Abstract
Shape 3

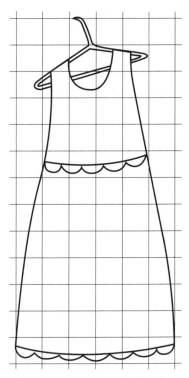

Paper-covered Wardrobe (page 52)
Grid Template

Abstract Cut-outs (page 50)
Enlarge to twice this size

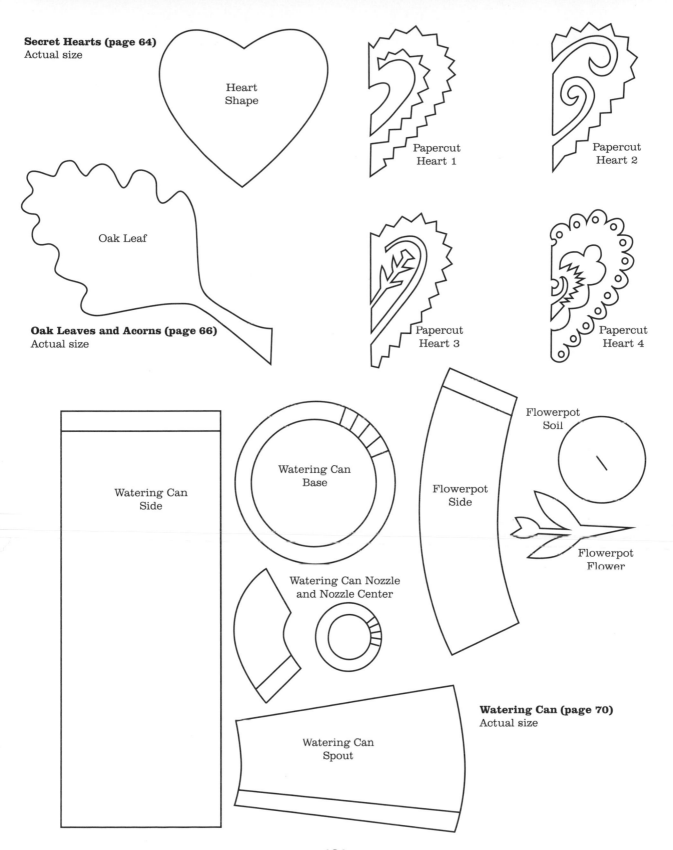

Secret Hearts (page 64)
Actual size

Heart Shape

Papercut Heart 1

Papercut Heart 2

Oak Leaf

Oak Leaves and Acorns (page 66)
Actual size

Papercut Heart 3

Papercut Heart 4

Flowerpot Soil

Watering Can Side

Watering Can Base

Flowerpot Side

Flowerpot Flower

Watering Can Nozzle and Nozzle Center

Watering Can (page 70)
Actual size

Watering Can Spout

TEMPLATES ✳

Vintage Papier-Mâché Dolls (page 76)
Actual size

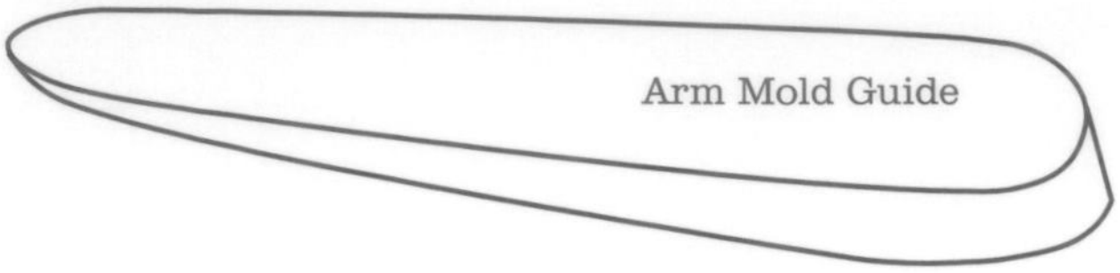

Arm Mold Guide

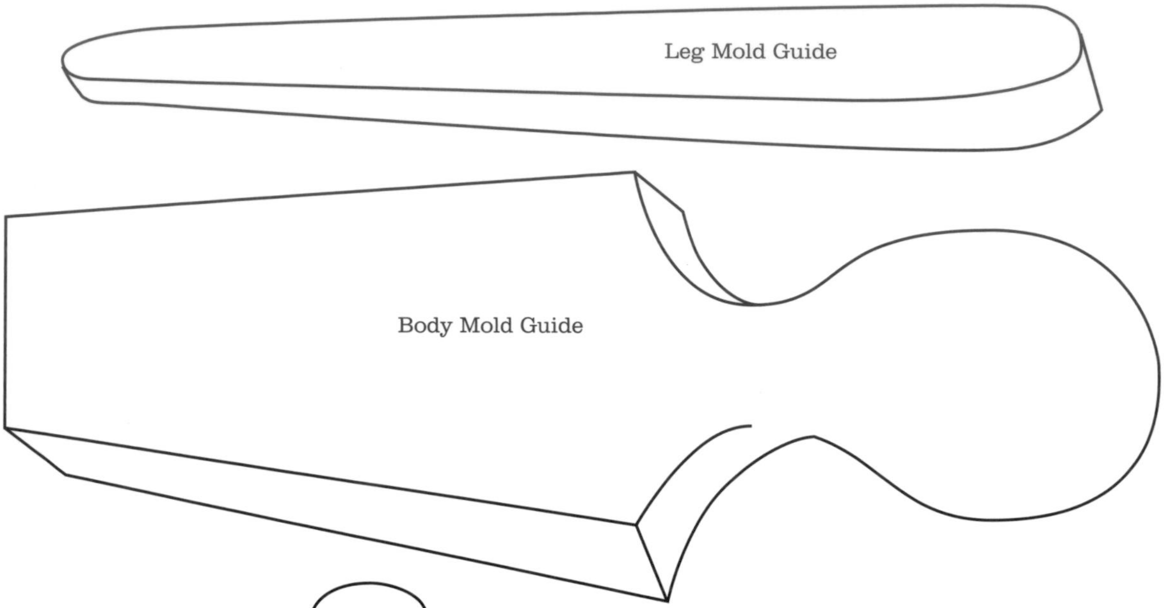

Leg Mold Guide

Body Mold Guide

Jumping Jacks (page 80)
Actual size

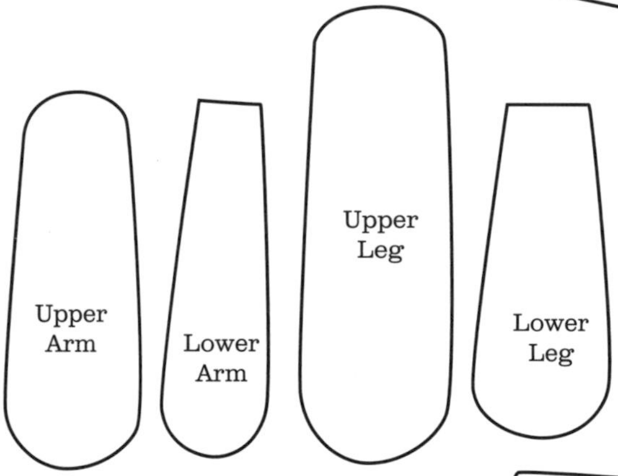

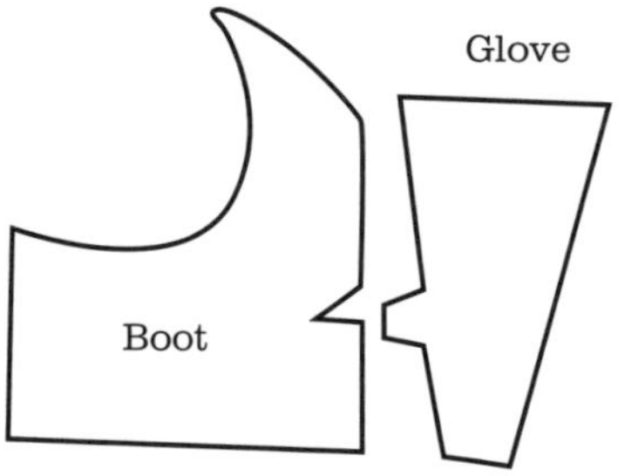

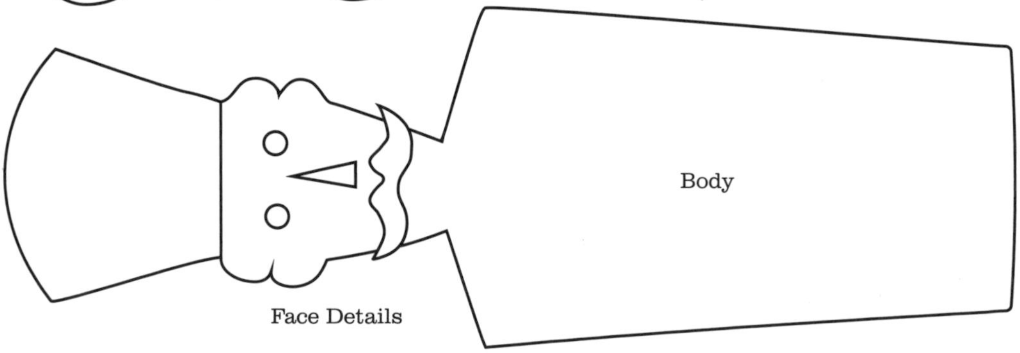

Glove

Upper
Leg

Upper
Arm

Lower
Arm

Lower
Leg

Boot

Body

Face Details

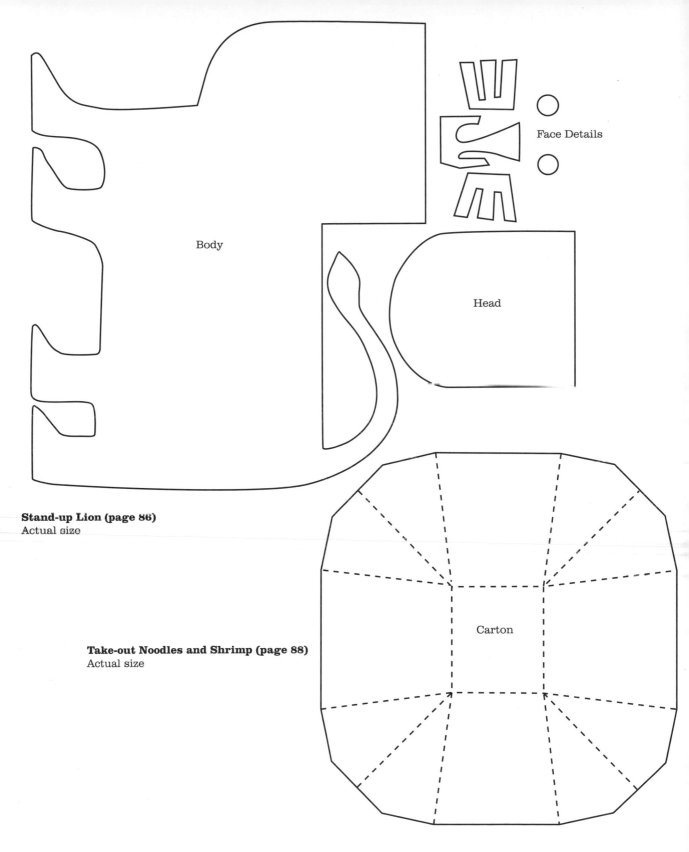

Body

Face Details

Head

Stand-up Lion (page 86)
Actual size

Take-out Noodles and Shrimp (page 88)
Actual size

Carton

TEMPLATES ✳

Wise Owl (page 96)
Actual size

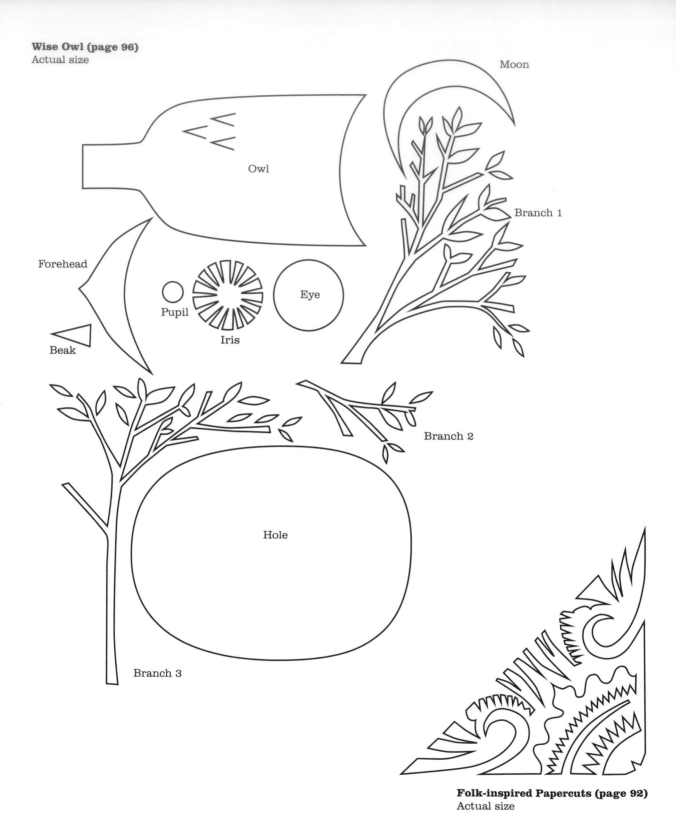

Moon

Owl

Branch 1

Forehead

Pupil

Iris

Eye

Beak

Branch 2

Hole

Branch 3

Folk-inspired Papercuts (page 92)
Actual size

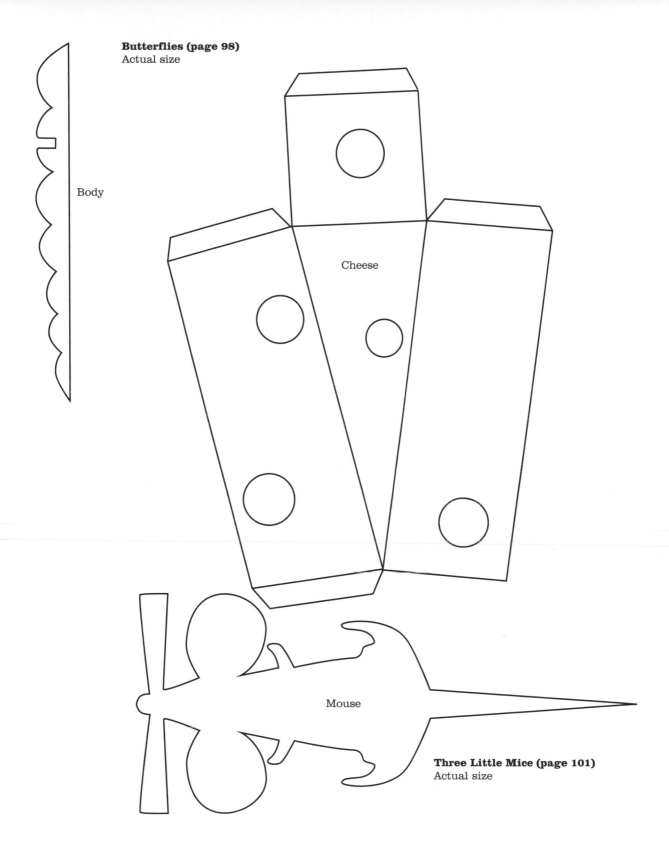

Butterflies (page 98)
Actual size

Body

Cheese

Mouse

Three Little Mice (page 101)
Actual size

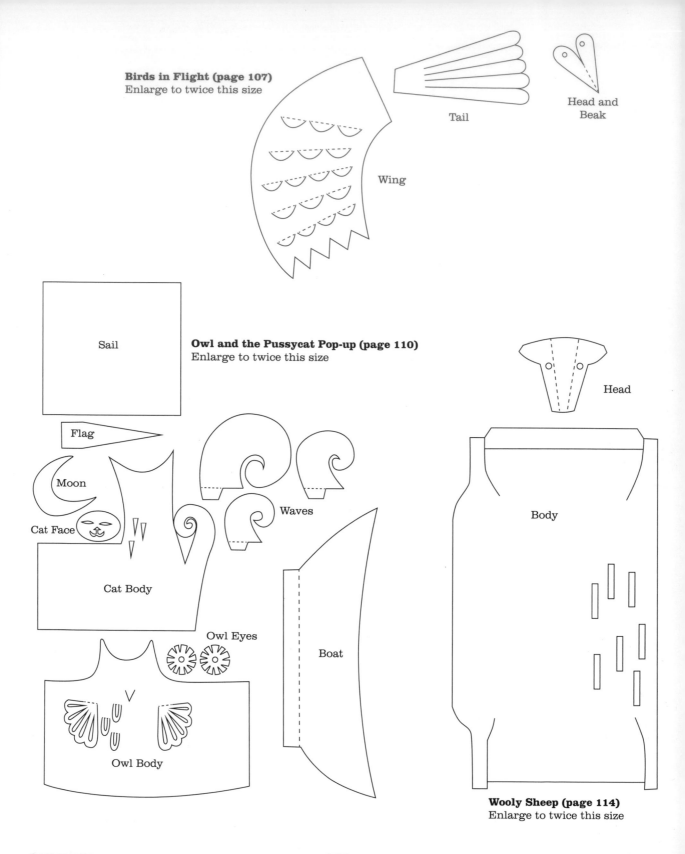

Birds in Flight (page 107)
Enlarge to twice this size

Tail

Head and
Beak

Wing

Sail

Owl and the Pussycat Pop-up (page 110)
Enlarge to twice this size

Head

Flag

Moon

Body

Cat Face

Waves

Cat Body

Owl Eyes

Boat

Owl Body

Wooly Sheep (page 114)
Enlarge to twice this size

Suppliers

UK SUPPLIERS

Cass Art
Stores across London
020 7354 2999
www.cassart.co.uk

Craft Creations
Online store
01992 781900
www.craftcreations.com

Crafty Devils
Online store
01271 326777
www.craftydevilspapercraft.co.uk

Falkiners Fine Papers
London paper store
020 7831 1151
www.falkiners.com

Hobbycraft
Stores nationwide
01202 596100
www.hobbycraft.co.uk

Paperchase
Stores nationwide
www.paperchase.co.uk

The Papercraft Company
Online store
07812 575510
www.thepapercraftcompany.co.uk

Papercraft 4 You
Online store
02392 318097
www.papercraft4you.co.uk

Total Papercraft
Online store
01702 535696
www.totalpapercraft.co.uk

US SUPPLIERS

A.C. Moore
Stores nationwide
1-888-226-6673
www.acmoore.com

Art Supplies Online
Online store
1-800-967-7367
www.artsuppliesonline.com

Crafts, etc.
Online store
1-800-888-0321
www.craftsetc.com

Craft Site Directory
Useful online resource
www.craftsdirectory.com

Hobby Lobby
Stores nationwide
www.hobbylobby.com

Jo-Ann Fabric and Craft Store
Stores nationwide
1-888-739-4120
www.joann.com

Kate's Paperie
Stores across New York
1-800-809-9880
www.katespaperie.com

Michaels
Stores nationwide
1-800-642-4235
www.michaels.com

Paper Source
Stores nationwide
www.paper-source.com

Index

Acknowledgments

Thanks to all at Cico for giving me the opportunity to work on such a lovely project, especially Cindy, Sally, and Pete, who are all such a pleasure to work with. A special thanks to Caroline for her beautiful and inspiring photography and to Charlie and Teo the designers who has created such a great look for the book. Thanks as always to my very lovely family Ian, Milly, Florence, Henrietta, and Harvey who are always there for me and give wonderful support, advice, and encouragement.

Kk Kk Yy Z

metick

& western England

Thomas

In Letter

martin Barbarity

PRTUW